THE ABC'S OF CHAKRA THERAPY

The ABC's of CHAKRA THERAPY

A WORKBOOK

Deedre Diemer   M.A., C.HT.

SAMUEL WEISER, INC.
York Beach, Maine

First published in 1998 by
Samuel Weiser, Inc.
P. O. Box 612
York Beach, ME 03910-0612

Library of Congress Cataloging-in-Publication Data
Diemer, Deedre.
The ABC's of chakra therapy : A workbook / Deedre Diemer
p. cm.
Includes bibliographical references and index.
(pbk. : alk. paper)
1. Chakras. 2. Healing. I. Title.
RZ999.D54   1998
615.8'52--dc21
97-51637   CIP
ISBN 1-57863-021-5
VG

Cover art and book design by Kathryn Sky-Peck
Illustrations copyright © 1998 Samuel Weiser, Inc.

Typeset in 10.5 point Garamond

Printed in the United States of America

03 02 01 00
10 9 8 7 6 5 4 3 2

The paper used in this publication meets the minimum requirements of the American
National Standard for Permanence of Paper for Printed Library Materials Z39.48-1984.

Contents

Acknowledgments |

I wish to express my heartfelt gratitude to all those who have support-ed and continue to support, encourage, and inspire me along this path of Self-transformation and healing:

My brother, George Diemer, for his generosity, humor and love; my aunt, Emma Lou Diemer, for her encouragement and creative genius; all those with whom I have studied, in person or through books, assisting me in laying the foundation for my spiritual growth *(please refer to the Recommended Reading List)*; my students and clients who have also been my greatest teachers—particularly those who inspired and participated in my first chakra therapy classes: Jenny Kamita, John Price, Anthony Michael Salas, Pat Hagan, Phyllis Jeroslow, Rachel Benioff, Coni Herndon and Laura Vallance. Blessings to Dina Tevas-Ingram for her enthusiasm, direction, and belief in the importance of this work. Much love to Julie Bradberry, my dear friend, and Sue Bottfeld, angel extraor-dinaire, who have both so generously given of their love, wisdom and spiritual support. My deepest love and appreciation to my beloved hus-band, Chris Pettersen, for standing by me with more faith, love, and devotion than I have ever experienced.

And of course, my greatest thanks to God, for allowing me to be a vehicle for this information.

And to all of you who are also on this wonderful journey, sharing your wisdom and heart—I honor you and thank you!

Part One

GETTING TO KNOW YOUR CHAKRAS

Welcome to the ABC's of Chakra Therapy!

If you've picked up this book, most likely you are already well on your path to Self-discovery and Self-healing. *The ABC's of Chakra Therapy* is designed to take you on a journey of becoming more of who you truly are (your higher potential) through the exploration of your main energy centers (chakras). These simple, yet powerful techniques are designed to facilitate healing on all levels—physical, mental, emotional and spiritual—through clearing blocks in your energy field, restoring your balance and energy flow. You will learn energizing techniques for charging and clearing out energy blocks, how to run your own energy, and have the opportunity to experience the transformational power of visualization, sound, color, aromatherapy, reflexology, crystals/gemstones, and physical exercise.

Through familiarizing ourselves with our chakras, we become more aware of what is our own energy and what is the energy that belongs to someone or something else. For example: has this ever happened to you? You're walking down the street feeling great, confident, and in a good mood. You pass a crowd of people or perhaps just one person—maybe you're aware of him or her, maybe you're not. Soon you find yourself thinking negative thoughts, maybe feeling angry, irritated. You wonder, "Where did that come from, I was just in such a great mood?" Sound

familiar? Well, you've just been "slimed"—you've picked up on the negative energy of someone in the crowd, and the energy penetrated your
aura so now you believe you're the one who feels awful, when the reality
is that someone totally separate from you just dumped his or her negativity on you, and you took it! When you're aware and certain of your
own energy, you'll know right away that you've taken on someone else's
energy (beliefs, thoughts, emotions, childhood programming, societal
programming, etc.) and by using any variety of the tools mentioned in
this workbook, you'll be able to clear your own energy to bring yourself
back to a more neutral state. From that neutral state, you are better able
to make decisions, see clearly what needs to be done; in short, you are
better able to take control of your life—no longer being at the unconscious effect of those around you.

There are several ways you can use *The ABC's of Chakra Therapy*. You
can explore each chakra individually, perhaps spending a week on each
chakra. Before you do anything, I recommend familiarizing yourself with
the basic skills mentioned later. Once you're familiar with the basic
skills, read the material for each chakra. For those of you who are more
auditory, you may want to create your own meditation tape by recording
your voice reading the Chakra-Related Emotional, Mental, and Physical
Health Issues for each chakra. Then listen to the corresponding tape, and
experiment with the alternative forms of therapy to find out which ones
resonate the most with you. Maybe all of them do, maybe only one, it
doesn't matter—trust yourself!

Included in *The ABC's of Chakra Therapy* is the Where is Your
Energy Blocked? section. This is a self-diagnostic that I've designed to
assist you in locating where your energies may be blocked. This self-diagnostic is quite extensive. You may or may not wish to answer all the
questions in one sitting. However, going through it once may assist you
in determining where your major blocks are—the ones that tend to
correspond with major life issues. After that, I suggest scanning the diagnostic to determine which questions seem to resonate with you at that
moment (questions that you answer "yes" to). Then check the answer
sheet to determine which chakras correspond with the question(s). Once
you discover which chakras are the most out of balance, you can use any

of the recommended therapies to assist in alleviating the blockage: i.e., listening to a corresponding chakra tape that will take you through a guided visualization, or breathing in the color that corresponds with the chakra, selecting an appropriate crystal and placing it on the chakra, etc. In my experience, the Running Energy Meditation is extremely powerful for raising your vibrational level and clearing blocks in your energy field.

How to Use the Different Therapies

Your Personal Guided Meditation Tapes (optional)

I strongly recommend the Running Energy Meditation as an extremely efficient way of clearing your energy field. You can sit and Run Energy on your own, or you can use one of the Guided Meditation Tapes that you can make to assist you with the clearing process of each chakra. You will want to set aside quiet time for this, as this is a meditation technique that requires focus and freedom from distractions. Do not listen to these tapes while driving your car, as you need to be focused and alert while driving!

Nature Therapy

Nature Therapy provides images and nature-setting suggestions that stimulate or relax the chakras. The best way to utilize this therapy is if you can meditate (sit quietly in contemplation) in the actual nature setting recommended. Sit by the ocean contemplating the sunset, sit outside in the moonlight, etc. The next best thing to do is to create a vivid picture in your mind and meditate on that, or perhaps find a photograph to meditate on. Use your imagination!

Sound Therapy

Sound Therapy is very subjective and I encourage you to listen to the music that resonates inside of you. There are recommendations in this book, however you are the best source of information as to what relaxes or energizes you musically. Explore different sounds and music. When you have a sense of the vibration that resonates for you and each individual chakra, I suggest making a tape for your listening and relaxing pleasure—perhaps five minutes of music or sound for each of the seven chakras. You'll be making a 30-minute tape (the sound for the 7th chakra is silence). You can sit and listen to the tape, or you could do the Running Energy Meditation while listening to it, or burn incense, etc.

Also included in Sound Therapy is vocal chanting. Whether you are vocalizing specific vowels or chanting mantras, allow the sound, the vibration, of your own voice to resonate and clear your energy! You don't have to be a singer to do this. We all have a voice—use it for your own healing!

Aromatherapy

Our sense of smell is a powerful tool for healing—releasing and relaxing. Use incense, potpourri, or essential oils designed for aromatherapy—again you can make this as elaborate or as simple as you want. I suggest starting simply. That allows you to find out if aromatherapy resonates with you before investing a lot of money in room diffusers, etc. I highly recommend combining aromatherapy with any meditation technique!

Color Therapy

Color Therapy involves visualizing and breathing the different colors into your energy field. This therapy, combined with the physical exercises and/or Running Energy offers a great clean-out! You can select the color corresponding to the chakra that is the most out of balance and breathe that color into that particular chakra and your aura; or you can take the time to sequentially explore your chakras and breathe the corresponding color(s) into each chakra. Again, use your creativity and imagination! Experiment with different colors. For example, while Running Energy, you might want to visualize a particular color above your crown chakra and let that color's energy flow throughout your energy field. Or perhaps you can wear clothing of a particular color to energize you—colored underwear is great, and if you can make it silk, it's even better! Many people will attest to the protective qualities of silk. Remember that white contains all the color spectrum, so it's always a safe choice. If you wish to activate a particular chakra, you may also want to surround yourself with the corresponding color: i.e., to activate the heart chakra you may decide to wear pink jewelry, place pink flowers around you, etc. Consider the color of your bed linens, surround yourself with colors that complement your energy and give you the results you're looking for. For example: orange-red may be great for sexuality/creativity, but may not be conducive to getting a restful, peaceful night's sleep!

Gemstone/Crystal Therapy

There is much to be said about the healing powers inherent in crystals, yet always remember that they, too, are just tools for healing. The ultimate source of healing is still within you—your Higher Self, whatever you wish to call it on a word level. Please be sure you don't give your power away to anyone or anything else (including crystals)! One way you can approach this form of therapy is to: lie down in a comfortable position (face up or down), place one corresponding gemstone or crystal per chakra on each of the chakra points on your body, and remain in that reclining position for approximately twenty minutes. This can be very powerful, depending upon how sensitive you are to the healing properties of the gemstone or crystal you select. Experiment to find out which crystals work for you, and know that your selection may vary, depending upon what you are experiencing in your life at the moment. Remember, one gemstone or crystal can be beneficial for more than just one chakra (i.e., clear quartz is a powerful healer for all the chakras).

Another approach is to carry those crystals or gemstones with you, or you may want to wear one. Due to the conductive qualities of gemstones and crystals, it is recommended that you "clean them out" prior to using them. One method I recommend is placing the gemstone or crystal in water and sea salt—ideally overnight. However, for a quick cleansing, holding them under running water will work. You can also burn sage and clean them with the smoke from the burning sage.

Reflexology

Just as there are hundreds of chakras in your body, so are there reflex zones that correspond with every organ of your body and reflex zones in your feet that correspond with the seven major chakras. In using this form of chakra therapy, a gentle, circular massage technique is recommended, using one, two, or three fingers. Remember that chakra therapy takes place primarily on an energy level, not necessarily the physical plane. Massage these reflex points on your own feet, or if you're fortunate enough to have a willing partner to massage these points for you, that's an added bonus! Again, be gentle. This isn't deep tissue bodywork! Feel free to use a lotion if you'd like, perhaps a lotion containing aromatherapeutic oils.

Yoga Therapy and Physical Exercises

Listed in this book are physical and breathing exercises designed to charge and open each chakra. You can use the exercises on an as-needed, individual basis for the imbalanced chakra, or you can execute them in sequential order, starting with the 1st chakra and completing with the 7th chakra. I have included a group of exercises that can be performed in a series (see pp. 147–155). If you practice them as a series, you can feel the energy build from exercise to exercise, culminating in a release in the 7th. My understanding is that the exercises are designed to be practiced in a series. To do the sequence in its entirety takes approximately fifteen minutes and is a great way to start the day! These exercises are yoga-like in their nature, so also included are possible yoga practices and postures for each chakra. I've found that integrating color breathing with these exercises can greatly enhance the experience and clearing of the energy field.

The ABC's of Chakra Therapy just scratches the surface of the healing possibilities available through conscious clearing of our energy field. If one or more of the therapies touched upon resonates deeply with you, I encourage you to do further research—read books, take classes. Please refer to the Recommended Reading List as a resource. These are some of the books that have assisted me. There is so much information available to all of us! And as always, use your discretion. *Listen to the truth inside of you!* Your heart, your wisdom will direct you to what you need. You will, however, be required to take the initial first step—which you obviously have!

An Overview
of the
Chakra System

B efore we start working together, let's discuss some of the various beliefs about chakras that you will read about. More and more information is becoming available about chakras and you may discover, as I have, that there are numerous explanations of how the chakras work. For example, there are differing beliefs regarding the direction in which the chakras spin. Some teachers say they all spin clockwise, others say counterclockwise; yet another source may say they alternate with the 1st, 3rd, 5th, and 7th chakras spinning in one direction, and the 2nd, 4th, and 6th chakras spinning in the other direction. You may read that chakras spin different directions in men and women, or that the chakras point up and down and not front to back. There are differing schools of thought regarding the colors of each chakra, as well as how many chakras there are, and their respective locations in the physical body. In my opinion, all these concepts are accurate and valid because each individual perceives things in a different way. The most important thing to remember is that you need to work with the information that resonates for you. With this in mind, I'm going to share the concepts this workbook is based upon.

You may be asking, "Why study the chakra system? What's the benefit?" The main purpose in working with and understanding the chakras

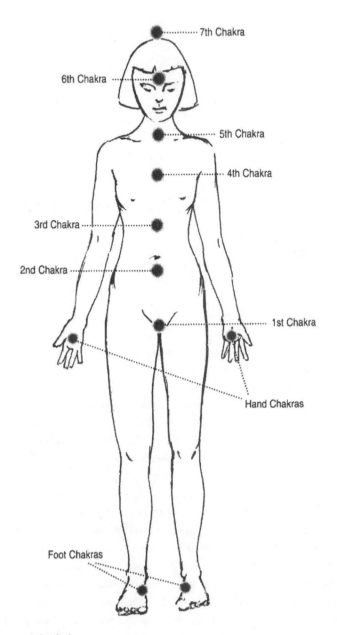

7th Chakra

6th Chakra

5th Chakra

4th Chakra

3rd Chakra

2nd Chakra

1st Chakra

Hand Chakras

Foot Chakras

Figure 1. The chakras.

is to create integration and wholeness within yourself. Knowledge of the chakras can be of immeasurable help in getting to know yourself. It can guide you in the realization of your inherent potential, and enable you to live a life full of abundance and joy.

The first major concept to understand is one of quantum physics—you are made of energy and sustained by energy. You do not end at your skin, your body is an ever-changing energy system that is affected by and affects the energy around you. Your physical body contains the most dense energy visible to the naked eye. This energy continues forming layers of energy fields around your body which are not usually visible, at least to the untrained eye. This magnetic energy field, shaped like an egg that surrounds your body is called your "aura." The aura is created by the energy of the chakras.

Chakra is a Sanskrit word meaning "wheel." A chakra resembles a spinning disc about the size of a silver dollar that opens and closes like the lens of a camera. Chakras are energy centers that receive and send information and life force energy; neuro-transmitters connecting nerves, hormones, and emotions. When a chakra is open, it is receiving information (picking up data from the environment around you). Generally speaking, whether a chakra is wide open or closed is not as important as whether the chakra system is balanced and the chakras are in alignment with each other. You may discover that the more open your chakras are, the more open you are as a person. Unfortunately in this world there still are situations when it may not be safe or appropriate to be too open, thus one goal is to become so in tune with yourself, through exploring your chakras, that you can consciously choose to open or close the chakras depending upon the situation.

Chakras actually appear in the astral energy body, but to make it easier to visualize where they are located, areas in the physical body are used as reference points. If that concept is challenging to accept, feel free to relate to chakras metaphorically. In actuality, your energy body contains hundreds of chakras, however, for our purposes we will focus on the seven main energy centers and two secondary centers referred to in figure 1 on page 10. The main chakras are connected to an "energy channel" that runs behind and parallel with the spine. All seven chakras affect each other and are interactive; much like any high-quality, fine-tuned instrument, so it is important that proper balance be maintained.

Each of the seven chakras correspond with particular body organs and emotional and psychological patterns. Physical illness and disease appear in the etheric body (energy system) prior to manifesting in the physical body. This being the case, I believe that our awareness of and ability to clear out our energy system can be a form of "preventive medicine," another great benefit from the understanding and exploration of your chakras.

In order to familiarize yourself with the individual properties of each chakra and provide a better understanding of how it might pertain to you personally, a brief overview of the seven main energy centers and the two secondary centers has been provided. Here you will learn the basics about each chakra's location and function, the mental, emotional, and health issues associated with that particular chakra, and what a "cord" in that chakra means. I will discuss "cords" in more detail in Part Two, but for now let me define "cord" as the following. Cords are lines of energy, resembling a string, that enter the chakra and connect you with another person. Basically, they are people's request for attention and can affect you deeply. This is a brief overview only. We will explore each chakra more fully in the Emotional, Mental, and Physical Health Issues section following the Self-Diagnostic.

Seven Main Energy Centers

1st Chakra
ROOT CHAKRA

Location: Base of the spine in men and between the ovaries in women.
Function: Sometimes called the "survival" chakra.

- Concerned with those mechanisms which keep the physical body alive: money, food, shelter;

- Family scars and social and familial information that form a person's idea of reality:
  - Includes immediate and extended family, race, social status, educational level, family legacy and family expectations as handed down through generations;
  - "Tribal mind"; concerned with loyalty—not love, kindness, or tenderness. "Love" being confused with obligation to the tribe: "If you really loved me, you'd come visit your family and me more often."

Cords: Cord in 1st means "I want you to help me survive."

Mental, Emotional Issues: Inability to keep a job or permanent living situation; lack of commitment; operating out of fear; need for safety/security in the world; not able to stand up for Self or to provide for life's necessities; unfinished business with parents; abuse or neglect in childhood; limiting psychological programming ("You're stupid," "You're a bad person").

Health Issues: Sciatica; varicose veins; chronic low back pain; rectal tumors or cancer.

2nd Chakra
SPLEEN CHAKRA

Location: Lower abdomen to navel area.

Function: Energy center through which we perceive other people's emotions (clairsentience);

- Concerned with day-to-day physical aspects of living; also with the people to whom we relate and with the quality of our relationships;
- Concerned with sexual energy and is the point from which we send and receive sexual feelings;
- Also concerned with creativity;
- Sometimes referred to as the "low heart" chakra in women.

Cords: Cord in 2nd means either, "I am interested in you sexually," or "Give me your emotional support, pay attention to my emotions."

- Sex cord can be left in depending upon whether or not you're enjoying it.
- Best to remove an emotion cord because it is a potential energy drain for you and is often accompanied by a "needy" vibration. (It's easier to respond to someone's emotional needs from your heart chakra than from your second chakra.)

Mental, Emotional Issues: Problems with money, sex and control issues with other people; blame and guilt; power or control in the physical world; emotional upset; fear of abandonment; sexual, emotional abuse/incest.

Health Issues: Sexual dysfunction; reproductive disorders; fibroid tumors; allergies; skin disorders; hemorrhoids; prostate and bladder problems; pelvic/lower back pain; over-indulgence in food or sex.

3rd Chakra
SOLAR PLEXUS CHAKRA

Location: Above the navel, below the chest.
Function: It is the body's distribution point for psychic energies—psychic energy pump;

- Power/control center: Will, personal power, authority, self-control, and self-esteem.

Cords: Cord in 3rd means "I want some of your energy, my own is not enough," or, "I'd rather operate on your energy than be responsible for running on my own."

- Cord in 3rd can also mean "I want to control you."
- Best to remove cord in the 3rd, as it can sap you of your own energy. A strong cord in this center can cause a tight sensation in your stomach.

Mental, Emotional Issues: Fear, intimidation; lack of self-confidence, self-respect, or self-control; inability to trust others; fear of assuming responsibility or making decisions for self; overemphasis on power/recognition; authority issues.

Health Issues: Digestive problems; indigestion; gastric or duodenal ulcers; anorexia nervosa; bulimia; pancreatitis/diabetes; colon/intestinal problems; arthritis; liver dysfunction; weight collected around the middle of the body.

4th Chakra
HEART CHAKRA

Location: Heart—center of the chest.

Function: The chakra of love, affinity, compassion and nurturance;
- "Oneness" with life: divine/unconditional love, forgiveness and openness;
- Sense of identity;
- Connects lower three physical/emotional centers to the three higher mental/spiritual centers;
- Sometimes referred to as "high heart" chakra in women— the "low heart" chakra being the second chakra (uterus /sexuality).

Cords: Cord in 4th means "I love you," or "I like you."
- May wish to remove cords in the 4th, if only for the sake of being the only person with energy in your body; however these cords aren't as draining as others.

Mental, Emotional Issues: Grief, issues with forgiveness, demanding judgmentality; unresolved anger, hostility, and criticism; self-centeredness; resentment, fear, bitterness; decrease in love of life; inability to give love to self or others; inability to receive love. If the "low heart" in a woman has been closed through rape, incest, or abuse, a woman cannot truly open her "high heart" until the wound has been acknowledged and the healing process has started.

Health Issues: Heart problems (congestive heart failure, myocardial infarction); emotional instability; problems with breathing; asthma, allergy; lung cancer; bronchial pneumonia; breast cancer; poor relationships; upper back, shoulder, or middle of the back pain.

5th Chakra
THROAT CHAKRA

Location: Throat area, at the base of the larynx.

Function: Chakra of communication, inspiration, personal expression, and following one's dreams;

- Center through which you receive your "inner voice"— clairaudience (clear hearing);
- Ability to receive nourishment—taking responsibility for one's personal needs;
- Power of the spoken word—speaking your "truth"—higher knowledge.

Cords: Cord in 5th means, "I want to communicate with you," and often, "I want to talk to you."

- Best to remove cord in the 5th, as a large cord in the 5th can cause an ache in the throat.

Mental, Emotional Issues: Issues with personal expression: inability to express one's true feelings, thoughts, and beliefs; inability to speak up for oneself; issues regarding following one's dreams and using one's power to create in the physical world.

Health Issues: Communication and/or speech problems; stuttering; thyroid problems; swollen glands; TMJ (temporomandibular joint problems); gum difficulties; throat and mouth ulcers; scoliosis; laryngitis; chronic sore throat; raspy throat; depression; shyness.

6th Chakra
THIRD EYE

Location: Center of the forehead, between the eyebrows.

Function: Clairvoyant (clear seeing) center, intuition, wisdom, personal vision;

- Is the chakra of visualization, imagination and insight;
- Another function is to let you know when other people are thinking of you, which is a form of "mental telepathy."

Cords: Cord in 6th means that someone is "in your head"—thinking of you intensely or wondering what you're thinking about, or perhaps what you think of him or her;

- Best to remove cord in the 6th as these cords can be the cause of headaches.

Mental, Emotional Issues: Fear of self-evaluation; intuitive skills and knowledge; misuse of intellectual skill; fear of being open to the ideas of others; paranoia and anxiety; refusal to learn from life experiences.

Health Issues: Eye problems; headaches; brain tumors; blood clots; neurological disorders; blindness; deafness; spinal difficulties; seizures; learning disabilities; tension; lack of concentration; sinus problems; mental confusion; lack of spiritual understanding or vision.

7th Chakra
CROWN CHAKRA

Location: Top of the head.

Function: Chakra of "knowingness" or pure intuition, seeing the larger purpose in our lives;

- Free will/ownership of body;
- Attitudes, faith, values, ethics, courage, and humanitarianism.

Cords: Cord in 7th means "I want to control you," or perhaps, "I want you to follow my teachings."

- Some gurus and religions place cords in the 7th so you'll follow the teachings of that particular guru, religion, group, etc.
- Some "spiritual" teachers will place a temporary cord in the 7th chakras of their students or disciples to facilitate learning.
- Remove cord in the seventh as it is tampering with your "free will."

Mental, Emotional Issues: Inability to trust life; issues with selflessness; inability to see the larger pattern in life; absence of faith; lack of inspiration; issues with humanitarianism; inability to make decisions; confusion.

Health Issues: Loss of free will; paralysis; bone cancer; skeletal problems; muscular system and nervous system diseases (multiple sclerosis and Lou Gehrig's disease); genetic disorders; fatal illnesses; brain problems; pineal gland disorders.

Secondary Chakras

There are two groups of secondary chakras that are found in the hands and feet.

FEET CHAKRAS

Location: Arch in the sole of the foot.
Function: Help maintain a person's connection with the Earth;

- Release old or stuck energy from the body.

Cords: Cord in your foot dislocates your grounding and may make you feel vague and spaced out or even "swept off your feet."
Health Issues: Ungrounded; inability to manifest practical reality; out of touch with reality.

HAND CHAKRAS

Location: Palm of the hand—center point between thumb and index finger.

Function: Seat of creative energy —comes into play when we make or do something;

- Healers use their hands both to receive and to communicate healing information and energy.

Cords: Cord in your hand may mean either "Do it my way," or "Do it for me."

- Cord in your hand can affect the ways in which you actualize virtually anything you do, from cooking to exercising to writing. . .

Health Issues: Creative blocks (artist's block); closed to receiving information about the world; inability to manifest reality; shut down creativity or healing; arthritis.

Where is Your Energy Blocked?

Now that you have some basic background information about chakras, I invite you to delve deeper by answering as honestly as possible, the questions in the following self-diagnostic. This self-diagnostic questionnaire is a tool I've designed to assist you in getting to know your chakras and discovering how some of the chakra-related issues may be playing out in your life. This information will enable you to locate where your energies may be blocked. The first step toward self-discovery and healing is knowing where the blocks to your healing are; then you can use any of the therapies mentioned later to assist in opening and balancing the chakras. Remember, your energy is constantly in motion and changes from day to day, so as you solve some problems and let them go (as we will discuss in the next section), you may find that you answer these questions differently. This self-diagnostic is quite extensive. There are 110 questions. You don't have to answer them all right away!

The answer sheet is found on page 30. You will notice that the question numbers relate to the column on the left. There are boxes on the page, and for Question 1, for example, you can answer yes or no in the column marked "1st" and also in the column marked "6th." This means that your answer to this question affects more than one chakra. If you answer "yes" to Question 1, then you will mark both "yes" boxes for that question. Don't worry about what the box means.

There is space at the bottom of the page to total up your answers. The totals should stay in the columns, so all "yes's" that relate to the 2nd chakra will be totaled at the bottom of the "2nd" column.

When you have completed the questionnaire, the columns with the most "yes" answers will indicate the chakra energy centers that are the most out of balance. Keep in mind that your answers will vary from day to day, moment to moment, depending on your mood, your experience, and other factors.

Because you may want to answer these questions more than once, you will find extra answer sheets in the back of the book. Remember, you don't have to answer all the questions in one sitting, however going through the questionnaire once in its entirety will assist you in determining where your major blocks are—the ones that tend to correspond with major life issues. After that, I suggest scanning the diagnostic periodically to determine which questions seem to resonate with you at that moment. (Questions to which you answer "yes.") Then check the answer sheet to determine which chakras correspond with the question(s).

I encourage you to be honest in your responses. Remember, there are no right or wrong answers. Avoid a tendency to over-analyze. In other words, go with your "gut instinct," the first answer that comes to mind when you read each question. Please be gentle with yourself, invoke your sense of adventure and fun, and enjoy what you may discover along the way!

SELF-DIAGNOSTIC

1. Do you feel lightheaded or "spacey"?

2. Have you recently experienced a situation where you felt that the rug had been pulled out from under you?

3. Are you more concerned than you used to be about meeting your monthly expenses?

4. Are you worried about not having enough financial security?

5. Are you suffering from constipation or diarrhea?

6. Are you eating more than usual, perhaps to comfort yourself?

7. Do you eat for no reason at all?

8. Do you have addictive /compulsive tendencies (e.g. food, sex, alcohol, drugs)?

9. Are you experiencing more anger/aggression at your place of work?

10. Do you feel run down or have low energy?

11. Have you recently changed or lost a job?

12. Have you recently lost a relationship or has your relationship recently undergone a change?

13. Have you recently undergone a life-threatening situation (e.g. earthquake, fire, flood, auto accident)?

14. Do you hate to sweat?

15. Do you hate to "feel" your body?

16. Are you frightened or anxious for no apparent reason?

17. Are you accident-prone? (Walk into walls? Falling down? Twisting ankle? etc.)

18. Do you feel you are overly sensitive to other people?

19. Do you take on other people's "stuff"?

20. Are you experiencing a creative block?

21. Have you gotten out of touch with your sexual feelings?

22. Do you regularly frequent night clubs, bars, etc. to confirm your attractiveness as a sexual being?

23. If you feel as if you are overweight, is the weight localized in any of the following areas:
    a) chest
    b) lower abdomen
    c) stomach (above belly button)
    d) hips and thighs

24. Are you ashamed of or feel guilty about your sexuality?

25. Are you uncomfortable being touched even by those you know?

26. Are you having more sexual fantasies than usual?

27. If you are a woman, are your experiencing any discomfort around your reproductive organs? Painful menstrual cycles? Bladder infections? Yeast infections?

28. If you are a man, are you experiencing difficulty in getting and/or sustaining an erection?

29. Do you have multiple sex partners at any one time?

30. Are you afraid of making a commitment?
    a) financial
    b) sexual
    c) emotional

31. Do you recall a history of "abuse" in your family?
    a) physical
    b) emotional
    c) sexual
    d) verbal

32. Are you fascinated with unconventional sexual practices (e.g., S&M, bondage, fetishes, pornography)?

33. Do you have a fear of being out of control?

34. Are you a "take-charge" kind of person?

35. Do you get upset when things aren't done "your way"?

36. Is change difficult for you?

37. Do you seek outside validation/approval as a measure of your worth?

38. Is it hard for you to relax?

39. Do you suffer from insomnia?

40. Are you someone who conforms to the "rules" around you?

41. Do you feel like you've been "kicked in the stomach"?

42. Do you have or are you prone to digestive problems (e.g. ulcer, gastroenteritis)?

43. Are you concerned about what others think of you?

44. Are you a control freak?

45. Do you feel disoriented/nervous when things don't go the way you planned?

46. Do your friends accuse you of not being spontaneous?

47. Do you need or like to categorize people to feel "safe"?

48. Do you have a strong fear of rejection?

49. Do you worry about being rejected?

50. Have you recently experienced a rejection of some type?

51. Do you overcompensate by being overly friendly—smile when you don't feel it?

52. Do you feel numb? Emotionless?

53. Do you feel as if there is a weight on your chest?

54. Do you have difficulty breathing?

55. Is your sense of who you are changing?

56. Are you unsure of who you are?

57. Do you tend to find yourself in unhealthy relationships and find it difficult to break away?

58. Have you recently had an encounter with someone who you felt totally invalidated you, your ideas, etc.

59. Are you so busy taking care of others that you haven't taken care of yourself?

60. Do you feel that you have to emotionally distance yourself from other people?

61. Do you have a sense of other people/situations pulling at you or draining your energy?

62. When people come to you with a problem, do you feel obligated to do more than just listen?

63. Are you a people pleaser?

64. Do you frequently suffer from sore throat, laryngitis or earaches?

65. Do you frequently suffer from clogged sinuses?

66. Do you stutter when anxious?

67. Are people always asking you to "speak up" or speak a little louder?

68. When you have the chance to share something meaningful, does your mind go blank when it's your turn?

69. Are you shy? Quiet?

70. When you think about expressing yourself, do you get a "lump" in your throat?

71. Do you fantasize about telling someone off, and not go through with it?

72. Do you judge yourself as stupid or not having anything worthwhile saying?

73. Do you believe, "If you can't say anything nice, don't say anything at all"?

74. Do you clench your jaws?

75. Do you grind your teeth?

76. Do you try to suppress what you feel, whether good or bad?

77. Do you try to suppress negative emotions and feelings?

78. Do you use words as a weapon (e.g., to deliberately cut someone down to size)?

79. Do you use words as a shield (e.g., to put distance between you and another person)?

80. Are you afraid of public speaking?

81. Are you afraid of speaking up?

82. Are you afraid of voicing a contrary opinion?

83. Do you frequently suffer from headaches?

84. Do you trust logic and rational thinking more than your intuition?

85. Do you overanalyze situations, problems, etc.?

86. Do you (sometimes? frequently?) feel like you are losing your mind?

87. Do you (sometimes? frequently?) get confused easily?

88. Do you have impaired vision?

89. Do you "lose your head" in trying (stressful) situations?

90. Are you predominately left-brained (linear, logical) thinking?

91. Are you surprised at events in your life that, in retrospect, were obvious to those around you who clearly saw the situation as it really was?

92. Do you "live in" your head all the time? (e.g., thinking about the sex instead of experiencing it? Or reading a book while exercising?)

93. Do you believe in only those things that can be validated by one of the five senses (sight, sound, touch, taste, smell)?

94. Do you wake up feeling exhausted even after a good night's sleep?

95. Do you feel like you're walking around in a fog?

96. Do you rarely recall your dreams?

97. Do you doubt your intuition or your hunches?

98. Do you doubt that you have a soul?

99. Do you believe that nothing survives after death?

100. Are you confused about your mission in life?

101. Are you concerned only with the here and now—the physical, material world?

102. Do you believe—*without question*—the teachings of any organized religion, church, philosophy, government?

103. Do you frequently rely on others to tell you what is right and wrong?

104. Do you frequently rely on psychics to give you direction? ("Tell me what to do," is different from, "Tell me I'm a good person," or "Validate what I already know.")

105. Do you believe you have no choices in life?

106. Do you search for your answers outside of yourself?

107. Do you believe that everything in life is destined to happen?

108. Do you believe that someone else has "the answer to life"?

109. Do you believe that the search for a spiritual life is a waste of time?

110. Are the majority of your actions/decisions motivated by any of the following reasons:

    a) fear of cutting off support (food, shelter, clothing);
    b) to gain approval;
    c) they "know better than you";
    d) to feel loved and accepted;
    e) afraid to disagree.

ANSWER SHEET

?#	1st		2nd		3rd		4th		5th		6th		7th	
	yes	no	yes	no	yes	no	yes	no	yes	no	yes	no	yes	no
1	☐	☐									☐	☐		
2	☐	☐												
3	☐	☐												
4	☐	☐												
5	☐	☐												
6	☐	☐	☐	☐										
7	☐	☐	☐	☐										
8	☐	☐	☐	☐										
9	☐	☐	☐	☐										
10	☐	☐												
11	☐	☐					☐	☐						
12	☐	☐	☐	☐			☐	☐						
13	☐	☐												
14	☐	☐												
15	☐	☐												
16	☐	☐												
17	☐	☐												
18			☐	☐										
19			☐	☐										
20			☐	☐										
'yeses' per column														

?#	1st		2nd		3rd		4th		5th		6th		7th	
	yes	no	yes	no	yes	no	yes	no	yes	no	yes	no	yes	no
21			□	□										
22			□	□			□	□						
23a							□	□						
23b			□	□										
23c					□	□								
23d	□	□	□	□										
24			□	□										
25			□	□										
26			□	□										
27			□	□										
28			□	□										
29			□	□										
30a	□	□	□	□										
30b			□	□										
30c			□	□	□	□								
31a	□	□			□	□								
31b			□	□	□	□								
31c			□	□	□	□								
31d			□	□	□	□								
32			□	□	□	□								
33					□	□								
'yeses' per column														

?#	1st		2nd		3rd		4th		5th		6th		7th	
	yes	no	yes	no	yes	no	yes	no	yes	no	yes	no	yes	no
34					☐	☐								
35					☐	☐								
36					☐	☐								
37					☐	☐	☐	☐						
38					☐	☐								
39					☐	☐								
40					☐	☐								
41					☐	☐								
42					☐	☐								
43					☐	☐	☐	☐						
44					☐	☐								
45					☐	☐								
46					☐	☐								
47					☐	☐								
48							☐	☐						
49							☐	☐						
50							☐	☐						
51							☐	☐						
52			☐	☐			☐	☐						
53							☐	☐						
54							☐	☐						
"yeses" per column														

?#	1st		2nd		3rd		4th		5th		6th		7th	
	yes	no	yes	no	yes	no	yes	no	yes	no	yes	no	yes	no
55							☐	☐						
56							☐	☐						
57			☐	☐			☐	☐						
58							☐	☐						
59							☐	☐						
60							☐	☐						
61							☐	☐						
62							☐	☐						
63							☐	☐						
64									☐	☐				
65			☐	☐					☐	☐				
66									☐	☐				
67									☐	☐				
68									☐	☐				
69									☐	☐				
70									☐	☐				
71									☐	☐				
72							☐	☐	☐	☐				
73									☐	☐				
74			☐	☐					☐	☐				
75			☐	☐					☐	☐				
"yeses" per column														

?#	1st		2nd		3rd		4th		5th		6th		7th	
	yes	no	yes	no	yes	no	yes	no	yes	no	yes	no	yes	no
76			☐	☐					☐	☐				
77			☐	☐					☐	☐				
78					☐	☐			☐	☐				
79							☐	☐	☐	☐				
80									☐	☐				
81									☐	☐				
82							☐	☐	☐	☐				
83											☐	☐		
84											☐	☐		
85											☐	☐		
86											☐	☐		
87	☐	☐									☐	☐		
88			☐	☐							☐	☐		
89											☐	☐		
90											☐	☐		
91											☐	☐		
92											☐	☐		
93											☐	☐		
94											☐	☐	☐	☐
95	☐	☐									☐	☐		
96											☐	☐	☐	☐
"yeses" per column														

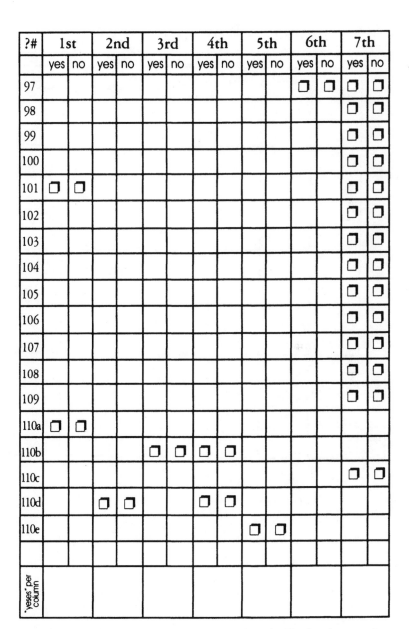

?#	1st		2nd		3rd		4th		5th		6th		7th	
	yes	no	yes	no	yes	no	yes	no	yes	no	yes	no	yes	no
97											☐	☐	☐	☐
98													☐	☐
99													☐	☐
100													☐	☐
101	☐	☐											☐	☐
102													☐	☐
103													☐	☐
104													☐	☐
105													☐	☐
106													☐	☐
107													☐	☐
108													☐	☐
109													☐	☐
110a	☐	☐												
110b					☐	☐	☐	☐						
110c													☐	☐
110d			☐	☐			☐	☐						
110e									☐	☐				
"yeses" per column														

*Note: A number of questions relate to several chakras. The chakras listed on the answer sheet are the chakras *most* affected. (Although other chakras may be affected to a lesser degree they have not been noted on the answer sheet.)

ANSWER SHEET TALLY

	1st	2nd	3rd	4th	5th	6th	7th
page 1 'yes' answers							
page 2 'yes' answers							
page 3 'yes' answers							
page 4 'yes' answers							
page 5 'yes' answers							
page 6 'yes' answers							
TOTAL all 6 pages							

Emotional, Mental, and Physical Health Issues

You have, like a majority of the people on this planet, beliefs, patterns of behavior, emotional upsets, and memories that for one reason or another you have chosen to put aside and deal with at "another time." In this section, Emotional, Mental and Physical Health Issues, I will be encouraging you to take a look at some of these situations, to examine what their roots are and to release them once and for all in order to facilitate emotional, mental, and physical balance, and to improve the quality of your life.

The first time you read this section, read it to gather information about chakra-related issues. Once you have learned the Basic Skills of Clearing Energy, which you'll find later in this book, I urge you to reread this section utilizing those skills. To take it one step further, I strongly encourage you to record this section for your own use. Read the text into a recorder, using your own loving and soothing voice, and create your own tape that you can use as a guided, closed-eye process while you practice the Running Energy Meditation.

In this section I will be suggesting probable scenarios of learned beliefs and behaviors that are related to the functioning of each chakra. Hopefully this will serve as a catalyst to jog your memory, allowing some of the hidden issues to surface, so you can look at them, release them, and heal.

This can be a tender process and I encourage you to be gentle with yourself. If at any time the process becomes too uncomfortable, please take a break, walk around, drink some water to regain your composure, *and start again*. It may be of interest to note that feelings of boredom or tiredness can indicate that you're starting to look at something you've been resisting, or that you may be on the verge of a breakthrough. To the best of your ability, keep going, but don't force the issue. These scripts are designed to be used with the Running Energy Meditation. When used in that format, because so much information is covered in the text, not much time is devoted to a single topic, which can make it challenging to delve deeply into any one issue. You can always make a mental note of the issue and look at it in depth at a later time after you've finished your meditation. There are times when just being aware of a situation or energy block is enough to release it. At those times digging deeper only encourages your holding on to the issue and prevents you from releasing it. Use your own discretion on this.

This text is not intended to be a substitute for personal, professional counseling. If something comes up that you don't know how to deal with, please take care of yourself and consult with a professional. You don't have to go through this alone. You can get support!

1st Chakra
ROOT CHAKRA

What are some of your beliefs regarding "survival"? "Man, it's a struggle to survive on this planet! It was so much easier when I was a kid. I really wish someone would take care of me. You've got to be tough in order to survive—it's a dog eat dog world. Money is scarce. I'd better move out of California before the Big One comes!"

Beliefs regarding your physical survival are associated primarily with the 1st chakra—issues regarding food, money, rent, shelter, natural disasters (earthquake, floods, fire, hurricanes, tornadoes, etc.), man-made disasters—anything that affects how secure and safe you feel in the world whether real or imagined! The 1st chakra is located at the base of the spine in men and between the ovaries in women. (Ladies, don't get hung up on trying to locate the exact position, trust yourself—your first chakra knows where it is!)

Much of what we believe about survival was learned when we were children. We learned from our parents, siblings, teachers, the media, society. This includes our immediate and extended family, our race, social status, educational level, family legacy, and our family expectations as they have been handed down through the generations. It is old programming that can be re-evaluated, released and replaced with our own set of beliefs that work for us now! Please remember as we explore our chakras that we need to "dissolve" any issues that come up. Please bring in LOTS OF FORGIVENESS and compassion! I recommend using the Running Energy Meditation (page 86), the transforming energy technique (page 92) and most importantly, the intention to release anything that can be released at this time, for the highest good—trusting your Higher Power!

First let's look at the survival of "our race"—whether it be "human race," White, Black, Hispanic, Asian, Female, Male, Catholic, Jewish, Protestant, Muslim, Buddhist, etc. A certain inherited "tribal mind" can be unconsciously passed on to us. We can see this most clearly in first- and second-generation immigrant families, for we see a sense of "clan"— holding onto traditions, beliefs from the "old country" that may not serve us in the present time. We have beliefs about obligations to the clan—loyalty—not necessarily love, beliefs about a woman's place in the family, in society, beliefs about a man's place. We also have beliefs about duty, surrender, and we may sacrifice our personal well-being for the good of the tribe. There are also beliefs we have assumed, but have not consciously chosen—"the family sticks together at all costs." This belief is dysfunctional in today's terms, and enforced by "enablers." We have denied any abuse, incest, addictions, corruption, etc., for the sake of the family name and social status. We have many wounds to heal in this area. These are issues to dissolve when we work with chakra therapy.

Perhaps you grew up in a household where money was scarce. So you learned to be very frugal—learned to penny pinch. Perhaps you learned that it wasn't okay to ask. Take a look at your permission level. Can you have what you want? Can you ask for what you want? If you can't, sometimes it relates to a survival level: as a child, you believed that if you asked for something and the request was denied, this was a personal rejection. Your survival appeared to be in jeopardy because if you angered or annoyed the family, you believed they might leave you and then you wouldn't survive. This is very real to a child. What was it like for you? (Keep dissolving the issues as they come up.)

Did you live in one house throughout your entire childhood? If you were fortunate enough to do that, take a look at it. What did you learn about change, new situations, movement? A majority of people moved several times. On the other hand, military families moved from location to location to location. Inherent with this lifestyle was never feeling rooted anywhere—life was transitory—you were transient. Did that affect your ability to get close to people, to maintain relationships? Take a look at your concept of "home." What is home? Home is probably much more than shelter. But in actuality the word home, a house, refers simply to a structure. What are all the conditions that have been attached to that word? Home is sometimes synonymous with security. No wonder there may be issues around the "homeless"—fear of becoming homeless, without security. What are your beliefs?

Relationships are affected by issues of survival. The 1st chakra is related to survival, to security, to your ability to feel safe. In many dysfunctional families (i.e., alcoholic parent, or an absentee parent), you as the child may have just started feeling secure when "wham!" the rug was pulled out from under you. The parent goes on a drunken binge, becomes abusive, or perhaps just withdraws inside him- or herself, or one parent physically leaves because of divorce, death, or extended absences. Survival. Did you learn to walk on eggshells at home? Were you ever allowed to feel secure? Parents, bless them, "loved" you and wanted the best for you, yet did you ever hear or sense this when you were feeling really happy, confident and solid? "All things come to an end. Don't feel too good, it's not going to last—the other shoe's going to drop." Parents' intentions were well-meaning, but what did that teach you? Did it teach you that you could never feel secure and happy for any length of time? Did you learn that someone could and would take your security away from you? Did you learn that security would affect your survival.

While we're exploring the 1st chakra, please remember to bring in some nice gold energy to cleanse the chakra. You may also want to breathe in the color red, which is the color therapy for the 1st chakra. Check for any cords in your chakra: remember a cord is a unit of energy from someone else that wants your attention. An energy cord in the first chakra has to do with survival. Somebody else may cord you saying, "I want you to help me survive." Now, let me make it very clear that being a parent and having a cord in your 1st chakra from your child is absolutely essential. Because up to a certain age, your child is dependent upon you for survival, and it would be inappropriate to remove that cord. (However, if your child is now 30 some years old and still cording you for survival, you may want to reevaluate. What's the mutual payoff?)

Do you have any beliefs that you have to take care of someone else? Your children? Your spouse? Your co-workers? Your parents? That's a tricky one! We all grew up believing that we could depend on our parents. Was that a reality? Did the roles reverse at some time and suddenly we started taking care of them? See if there are any unspoken agreements between you and your parents. Do you have a belief that in their old age you are responsible for them? Do they cord you in the 1st chakra because they need you for survival, or think they need you for survival? Again, it's your decision as to whether or not you want to remove an energy cord. I very much recommend removing cords, cleaning those people's energy out, because you need all your energy for your own survival. Once you have access to all your energy, then you can be available and more capable to assist others. When we are corded, our energy field gets clogged and we can't manifest as easily. We don't function with as much clarity, focus, awareness and self-confidence.

We "ground" or connect ourselves to the Earth through the 1st chakra. Do you have any beliefs, conceptions about being connected to this planet? That it's a punishment? Not spiritual? In my experience, the more "grounded" I become, the easier it is to access the spiritual information and bring it forward onto the Earth. Find the healthy balance—like the negative and positive charges of a battery. You need both positive and negative charges for the battery to work. So, too, we need Spirit as well as the physical to accomplish what we need to accomplish on this planet.

As you become more "grounded," people will attempt to "ground" through you. This is very common in relationships, particularly sexual relationships, where you ground through each other for more stability. That's just part of being human, and it's okay—to a point. Once you become aware of the cord, it's best to take back your grounding, send back the other person's energy and have that person ground through him- or herself. Allow your partner the opportunity to ground *through the planet* and not through you. If someone grounds through you, then you may always feel responsible, and it is a nagging sense of responsibility, restriction, and obligation.

Now, someone grounding through you was mentioned, but what if *you* ground through someone or something else? For example, many people ground through their work. Anytime our survival is threatened, fear comes up, and we tend to react out of fear. So, if you're grounding through work or someone else as a source of survival, this sense of fear will continue to exist because that job, that person or that something *outside of you* may die, leave, or be taken from you. I can't stress enough the importance of grounding for yourself, through yourself, through the planet Earth, to the center of the Earth. We've all seen people who operate out of fear—they lack grounding. They're scattered, spacey and nervous. Unfortunately, many actors, artists, commission-based sales associates and beginning entrepreneurs may have many survival issues to contend with: "When's my next gig? Will they like me? What's going to happen? Did the show sell? Are they going to pay me? Is the deal going to close?" Know that if you ground through anyone, anything else, you're undermining your ability to create for yourself, or to feel secure, or to trust. The 1st chakra is associated with primordial trust. When you trust that Mother Earth, the Universe, God, Supreme Being (whatever you call it on a word level) will always provide, you feel more secure and confident.

How much permission do you have to receive what you want? Again, this may have to do with the information we learned as children. Is it okay to receive? Is it okay to be abundant? Were you sent mixed messages? For example: You knew darn good and well there really was enough money to go around, yet your family always operated from a place of lack? Or was it the other extreme? Over-indulgence—spending more money than was available and then always playing catch up. Take a look at what the mood was around money, abundance, "havingness." What were the messages you received? It's one thing to spend money on something needed: to learn to trust that the Universe always provides what we truly need. It's another thing if you learned to overspend and then spiral into guilt, blame, resentment, fear, or anger when the money isn't there to cover the bills. It's beneficial to learn to be realistic in terms of saving money so you can live. However, it sometimes reaches a point where "save, save, saving" out of fear, leads to mistrusting that the Universe provides, then you end up depriving yourself of having your needs met.

The 1st chakra is a great chakra to explore, because it deals with so many issues: all the different money issues. Everyone on this planet has money and abundance issues in one form or another. Think of money as only one form of abundance. Money is only energy, a piece of paper providing an exchange of energy. That's all it is. Look at your issues around money. Are you getting paid what you are worth, realistically? Do you value yourself? If you are in a service-oriented occupation, have you agreed to an unspoken understanding that because you are of service that you aren't going to get paid what you deserve? That it's an honor? Some non-profit organizations have been known to operate from this agreement level—just check it out for yourself.

Abundance—self-worth—value: what did you learn about your worth as a human being, your value as a human being? Did you learn that you had to achieve a certain "something" before you could reap the rewards of abundance, prosperity, acceptance, and love? Do you hold a carrot out in front of you that says, "Well, as soon as I do this, I can be prosperous and have this"? Do you always put it off? Is the condition something intangible, so of course you couldn't accomplish it? Have you bought into statistics? Are you doing what you love? This all has to do with worth, connection to the earth. Primordial trust. Remember, in order to manifest on this planet, you must be connected (grounded) to it!

What concepts did you learn about food? Food is a part of survival. Did you learn that food was scarce? That you had to eat it fast or it might be gone? Take a look at your beliefs. What about "proper etiquette"? Having to eat, perfectly. "You must chew your food X number of times before you swallow!" "Never eat dessert first!" As a child, did your mother, babysitter, or sibling stuff food in your mouth to "shut you up" when you cried? Did you learn that food is a sedative and makes you feel better? That if you're upset, then you need food to take away the pain? What is it about food that you like? If it were just the nutrients, that would be fine. There's also texture, temperature, taste—what qualities from food do you associate with your well-being? Do you crave a particular food dish that your mother used to make for you as a child when you're feeling insecure? Pasta? Bread? Jell-O? Vegetables? The squeakiness of mushrooms or tomatoes? What ideas and beliefs have you formed? Dissolve any issues and judgment you may have about the way you look, about your body and how it functions. Have you bought into any form of eating that does not necessarily agree with you? Vegetarian? Meat-Eating? Bingeing? Purging? Fasting?

Reading this may have brought up some stuff for you— it's designed to do that. With awareness you can start to release and clear out your energy field. It's important to clear these patterns that have been brought to your attention because stuck energy or energy blocks set the stage for physical illness. Some of the health issues (physical, mental, and emotional) associated with the 1st chakra are as follows: sciatica and varicose veins—inability to stand up for yourself; chronic lower back pain—feeling a lack of support; rectal tumors/cancer—guilt, remorse over the past, an inability to "let go." These are just some of the issues associated with the 1st chakra. I encourage you to continue to explore on your own, being aware of any judgments that you or anyone else has placed on the issue. When you become aware of a judgment, please bring in forgiveness. It may not be possible to actually forgive the person or event, but it certainly is essential to forgive yourself and love yourself. Then the healing can take place.

2nd Chakra
SPLEEN CHAKRA

SEX! PASSION! GREED! LUST! DESIRE! Relationships! Addictions! Violence! Rape! Incest! Deception! Emotional Upset! Creativity!! Ah, the 2nd chakra—the stuff daytime television is made of! As a matter of fact, up to this point, our society operates predominantly out of 2nd chakra energy. Don't get me wrong, when the 2nd chakra is healthy and balanced in an individual it is a wondrous, powerful, creative, life-giving and artistic energy. And when it is imbalanced, it can produce equally destructive energy! There are many "spiritually-oriented" people who have wrestled with the 2nd chakra in their efforts to ascend and transcend the physical. It is a chakra that demands attention. So, now that your 2nd chakra issues are coming up to the forefront, let me remind you to be gentle with yourself. Dissolve issues as they come up and please bring in lots of forgiveness and love! You might also consider breathing a clear orange and/or gold color into your chakra as you proceed. Set your intentions to release what is ready to be released with grace and ease, for the highest good of all concerned.

The 2nd chakra, located in the lower abdomen, contains stored memories, emotions, and information about how you relate to other people, the quality of your relationships, the day-to-day physical aspects of living, the use of your sexual/creative energy. It is the energy center through which you perceive other people's emotions. The pelvic and reproductive organs are located in this area, and are, thus, along with the lower back, the organs most susceptible to disease when there is a blockage or imbalance in the 2nd chakra.

During childhood we developed our beliefs about ourselves, our sexuality, and our role as creative, emotional, sensual beings on this planet. It's also helpful to remember, just as in the 1st chakra, many programs that we learned during childhood were designed to benefit the "tribal mind." As such, many of us unconsciously moved into our roles in the 2nd chakra. Perhaps we chose partners that fulfill the needs of the 2nd chakra—marrying for physical security, money, children, social status, or fear of abandonment.

What did you learn about sex, sexuality, and sensuality? Did you learn to be proud of your sex or gender? Were you valued as a sexual being? What was it like during puberty? Were you self-conscious? Excited? Anxious? Ashamed? What was the atmosphere around your first menses? Your first erection? Were you frightened, or did you understand what was going on? Perhaps you didn't know what was happening to your body and felt afraid, ashamed, or confused. Newly racing hormones creating all those foreign feelings! Was anyone there to help you through this? Did the parent that you were so close to suddenly back off from you as you started developing into adulthood? Little girls no longer able to sit on daddy's lap. Little boys no longer able to hug and kiss daddy? Mommy? Were you treated differently? Told to play differently? "You can't play on the jungle gym anymore. Young ladies don't act that way!" "You can't play with that doll or toy stove. Boys don't do that!"

Were you shamed for being proud of your developing body? Breasts—pubic hair—were you proud of your newfound body? Did either of your parents compete with you, suddenly becoming threatened by your impending adulthood? You were no longer a child, so perhaps you got the message that it was not okay to be sexual, it was not okay to develop because they didn't want you to grow up. How did this affect your development? Did your body develop, or did it receive a message to hold back and retain a child-like physique? Perhaps it wasn't okay to be a female and you learned to run male energy—to be aggressive and get recognition. So you had to remain trim, breasts didn't fill out, thighs and hips didn't develop until later in life. For you men, were you allowed to develop your body? Were you encouraged to be sensual? Was it okay that you enjoyed sensual things—the touch of that beautiful silk pillow, that scarf, the fur, the leather— or were you humiliated? The belief that it's okay for little girls to play dress up and wear mommy's clothes, but if a boy did it, it was wrong or worse yet, perverted.

Were you sent messages that it's not okay to be the sex you are? If you are a woman, did you receive messages that in order to succeed in this world, you have to be a man, so you started hating being a woman in a woman's body? If you are a man, did you receive messages from your mother about how much she hates men, that men are jerks? What message did that give you: "Men are jerks, but I'm a man, does that mean I'm a jerk? Please love me even if I'm a guy?" Then did you go out of the way to please mommy to prove you're not a "jerk like all the rest of the men." For you ladies, did you constantly try to win your father's approval, but you never quite got it, because he did not know how to interact with a woman, a girl? So perhaps you chose the only thing you could think of—be more "male-like." Unfortunately, you still didn't get the approval you were seeking. Or maybe you got tons and tons of approval for being the "perfect child"—the cute one, the performer, the achiever, daddy's little girl, momma's good boy, the perfect angel. These are all things that you store in your 2nd chakra. That's why it's so important to clean these memories out.

Was sexuality openly talked about in your family? Was it a source of awkwardness or embarrassment, or even total denial and rejection? Was sex considered to be impure, dirty? Something bad? Something to hide and giggle about with your friends? Were your parents openly sexual and affectionate? Did they let you know that they were sexual beings? Did they let you know that it's okay and healthy to be a sexual being? Were you subjected to inappropriate sexual behavior? Did someone cross that boundary? Did someone touch you in a way that you didn't want to be touched, but you felt helpless to do anything about it? Perhaps you were a child when this happened, perhaps an adult. Or maybe you felt emotionally incested. Did you have a seductive, needy parent? Did you learn to turn off your feelings in order to survive? Feelings and emotions stem from the 2nd chakra—sadness, anger, rage as well as incredible joy and lightness! Give yourself permission and the safe space to feel your emotions. Then let go of the shame, anger, and rage so you don't use them against yourself. Please remember to take care of yourself, bring in forgiveness and compassion when needed, even if you don't think it's necessary.

We learned about relationships from parents and family. What is your image of relationship? What does relationship look like to you? Did you learn dysfunctional or healthy relationship skills? Chances are, like many of us, you learned dysfunctional ways of relating. Who did you attract into your life? Who do you attract in your life now? Have these people been supportive? Have they been abusive? Maybe they have not been abusive physically, but some people are mentally or emotionally abusive, eroding away at your self-esteem. Do you tend to place your partner's needs before your own? Were you accepted or were expectations placed upon you by your partner? You have to look a certain way, talk a certain way— did you feel accepted or judged? Or both? What part of you allowed that? Allow that part to come forward and release it. Dissolve anything that supplies energy to a limited belief regarding the types of relationships that you can have. This includes work-related relationships, friendships, not just sexual relationships. What is your relationship to the world, to animals, to money, to YOU? It's all relationship.

How do you relate to others? Do you sometimes feel what the other person is feeling? Do you find it difficult to be in large crowds without feeling overwhelmed and exhausted? Do you or others consider you to be a "sensitive" person? The 2nd chakra is also the chakra for clairsentience—the ability to perceive and oftentimes actually experience other people's emotions. There's good news and bad news regarding this ability. Yes, you can be very accurate in reading people, however the price you pay may be exhaustion, weight gain through the hips, thighs, abdomen and buttocks (your body's way of protecting you) and an inability to discern your true emotions from those of others. See if this rings true for you: you're "counseling" a friend in need—when the conversation starts you feel happy, energetic and clear. By the end of the conversation your shoulders are slumped forward, you feel drained and depressed, whereas your friend feels great and thanks you profusely, remarking how he or she always feels better after talking with you. Your "friend" just dumped on you, corded you in the 2nd chakra and now you're carrying the emotional garbage. Now's when you need to make separations and clean out the chakra. It's easier to counsel through the heart chakra, which is a higher vibration, providing a greater ability to remain neutral rather than matching the person in his or her 2nd chakra emotions.

Energy cords in the 2nd chakra usually indicate either: "I'm interested in you sexually," or, "Give me your emotional support, pay attention to my emotions." Sex cords can be left in for a while, depending on whether or not you're enjoying it. Sometimes it's valid: you probably would welcome a cord from your "romantic/sexual partner." This allows you to feel a sexual connection. However, once the urge has been filled, it's a good idea to decord and give back each other's energy. On the other hand, an emotional cord in the 2nd chakra is a potential energy drain and is often accompanied by a needy vibration and should be removed.

How do you relate in the world? When in your life are you run by your 2nd chakra? Are you with a person who's very emotional, needy and likes to hook you sexually? The "bar scene" is a perfect example of 2nd chakra interactions. The flirtatious remark? A sexual come-on. Do you manipulate others through your sexuality? Do you use your sexuality to land the job, close the deal, or make the "right" connection? Remember, there are no judgments here. If you felt one come in, take a deep breath and bring in forgiveness! The acting profession is filled with people who are struggling to balance 2nd chakra energy: that might be one reason they chose to act—it's a great way to get in touch with, express and release those emotions. And again *the key is balance!*

Extreme emotional highs and lows as a way of life possess an addictive quality. (You may have heard the term "drama queen"?) Anything used to alter the mood has potential for becoming addictive: thus it is in the 2nd chakra where you will find dysfunctional relationships to alcohol, food, drugs, sex; under which lies the addictive need for approval.

When the 2nd chakra energy is balanced, a positive creativity can take place. Artwork, novels, music, and perhaps the most miraculous and awe-inspiring creation—giving birth to a new life. Anger can be redirected into passion—passion for life and creation. If you deny yourself a creative outlet, your energy centers can become blocked, you become depressed, and that's when physical disease has a greater chance of manifesting: reproductive disorders, fibroid tumors, cervical cancer, prostate cancer, hemorrhoids, bladder disorders, allergies, pelvic and lower back pain, and sexual dysfunction.

The 2nd chakra contains a wealth of information for each of us and I encourage you to further explore the issues that have been uncovered for you—at your own pace. Please keep in mind that the lower three chakras are considered to be on the "physical level" and as such can appear to be very heavy and a bit overwhelming at times. Have patience with yourself, your process, and trust in your Higher Power to guide you. The clearer the energy field, the easier it is to receive inner guidance. Acknowledge and appreciate yourself for your courage and willingness to be on this path of learning and self-growth.

3rd Chakra
SOLAR PLEXUS CHAKRA

Control—power—boundaries. What images do those words conjure up for you? Who has control? Do you? Does someone or something else? Who gave them that control, that power? What happens when someone else is in control? Do you feel helpless? Angry? Resentful? Victimized? Our society thrives on power, over-emphasizing both it and recognition—it's power driven. Look at the government, the military, the IRS, the legal system, the Fortune 500 corporations, Wall Street, terrorists, prisons, jails, our educational system.

Please remember to visualize gold energy as you explore the 3rd chakra. Bright sunny yellow is the color therapy for this chakra, so you may also find it beneficial to breathe that color into your chakra. The issues associated with this chakra can be rather intense and bring up a lot for you, so as always, please be gentle with yourself. Take your time, ask that anything that can be released, be released for the highest good. As issues come up, dissolve them. Take care of yourself, and if something is uncovered that you do not want to deal with on your own, please reach out and seek professional assistance.

Our personal sense of control, or lack of it, is associated with the 3rd chakra. Reflect a moment: have you ever experienced a situation where you were confronting an authority figure or in the middle of a power struggle? Where did you feel it in your body? Most likely in the stomach—a burning, tightening sensation that can also feel like you've been punched in the stomach (and you have, energetically speaking). In martial arts this is where "chi" is located—the center of harmony and groundedness. For all sports activities and physical fitness, the importance of developing strong rectus abdominus muscles is highlighted. All movement—physical and energetic—passes through this center.

If this energy center is blocked there may be a challenge integrating emotions with the heart which can then translate into criticism and judgment. The 3rd chakra is the bridge between the 2nd (emotions, sexuality, creativity) and the heart (unconditional love, identity). When the energy is flowing freely, you're in touch with your heart and compassion, having greater understanding and empathy for yourself and others when feelings surface. Take a look at some of your sexual relations—the experience of sex without love can be a by-product of a blocked 3rd chakra. Feeling uncomfortable and judgmental when watching someone else express feelings, or feeling cold and distant inside yourself is also indicative of a blocked 3rd chakra. "Who cares about your crummy emotions?" Allowing emotions to come forward can create a fear of being out of control if there is a belief that emotions are so powerful they will take over and you'll never resurface.

What situations create the sensation of being out of control for you? Roller coaster rides? Plane rides? Alcohol? Food? Sex? Drugs? Love? The workplace—not wanting to delegate because no one else can do it "right"? So, instead you overextend yourself as a way to validate yourself, to keep control over the environment. That intense need to control your limited environment—hold on tightly if you perceive the situation slipping out of your control. What about the overbearing boss, the "control freak," breathing down your neck, belittling you, overly mindful of your work load—prompting you to feel as if you have no control? Organizations of the Big-Brother-is-watching-you type, which promote feelings of helplessness, hopelessness, and resentment—jails, prisons, institutions, some schools where everything is structured, no privacy, strict rules, regulations, punishments, no freedom. Perhaps you experienced this during your childhood.

Imagine, if you will, being a child. Before you knew limitations, you were free! You were a joyous, loving being looking at the world with wonder and awe. It was your world—the universe according to you! Then pretty soon you started hearing the words, "no," "can't," "don't!" Your little face started scrunching up, turning red, fists clenched, stomach tightening as you cried out in frustration, anger, confusion, and rage. Or perhaps, you were a child left in an incubator, or felt the restrictions of too tight swaddling, or a cast on part of your little body. Perhaps you learned to control the environment through your temper tantrums. Eventually you may have given up and figured that the best way to control your surroundings was by pleasing the big humans, seeking their approval. That worked for a while. You learned to seek approval as a means of getting what you want. Very ingenious. Except the outcome of that behavior still brought about a sense of being out of control because you weren't allowed to be yourself, to have your honest responses. Certainly we weren't allowed to have our rage, so not only did we shut down our 2nd chakra, we also shut down our 3rd.

Let's take this to the next step. Your parents were the ones to initially lay down the rules. And they did that with the best of intentions. It comes with the territory of being a child on this planet. Yet other authority figures entered the picture. What was your experience of school? Sunday school? Did you have any teachers who abused their authority? The horror stories (real or imagined) of the nuns and headmasters with rulers and paddles? The embarrassment and humiliation suffered at the hands of an impatient teacher? Were you singled out and made to feel wrong if you didn't conform? Maybe you had a strong spirit and could tolerate "sitting in the corner" or being "sent to the principal's office" for "bad behavior." Are you now someone with a rebellious streak—still refusing to conform? Or did you feel intimidated so that it was hard to speak, thinking that the teacher had all the power? Did you learn to disappear—daydream? Fantasy is one way to control your world—create it in your mind to escape reality. Were you at the mercy of someone else's moods? Teachers, parents, family—what authority figures today do you have issues with? Police, politicians, lawyers, doctors, government agents, priests, rabbis, the Pope, your guru, your boss, your spouse, parents?

Take a moment and sense if there are any cords in your 3rd chakra. If there are, what's the message carried by the cord? Is it: "I want to control you," or maybe, "I want some of your energy, mine is not enough." Those people who do not want to take responsibility for themselves may try and cord you in the 3rd so they can run on your energy, because "I don't want to be responsible for what I do but if I hook into your energy, you've got pretty cool energy, I know you'll take responsibility for me." It's called co-dependent behavior, addictive behavior. It's no accident that the umbilical cord just happens to be located in the 3rd chakra. Is mom still tied to you? Are you still tied to mom? Are you letting her run your life, seeking her approval? Maybe mom was more subtle about her control whereas dad was the blatant one. Are you passive-aggressive? Passive, nice, understanding until you can't take it any more and then you lash out? Or you stuff it all. Or you let it out while driving on the freeway—now that's a frightening one, and we've all probably done it—used our vehicles to express the frustration at being cut off in traffic, or, "I'm not letting you in buddy, who do you think you are? Nobody let me in. . . ." Ah, the 3rd chakra freeway-of-life.

What did this teach you about control in relationships? The umbilical cord is where you had the parental relationship, which then colors all further relationships. Whatever we learned in that 3rd chakra, we recreated time and time again, until we learned how to relate adult to adult. If we have learned. Using the terminology of transactional analysis, what are the dynamics of your relationships? Are you always the parent (in control) over the child? Nurturing, taking care of, educating, possibly feeling superior to your partner, co-workers or friends? Or do you assume the child role: "Take care of me. I don't want any responsibility. I give you my power. Lead my life for me." Perhaps you switch off from parent/child to child/parent? Again, no judgments here—please bring in lots of forgiveness and compassion. We learned to copy the only role model we had for relationship—our parents' relationship with each other and our relationship with our parents. It has to be a conscious, learned ability to relate on an equal basis—adult to adult.

What about when you receive news that's hard to digest? The declaration: "I just feel sick about that happening." Do you get so upset about something that you can't eat? Holding onto stress? Ulcers? All these are related to 3rd chakra imbalances—digestive problems, indigestion, colon and intestinal problems, pancreatitis or diabetes, liver dysfunction. Anorexia nervosa and bulimia relate to low self-esteem, and feeling so out of control that the only way to control is by slowly killing or starving oneself. You can easily spot a man preoccupied with control because of the extended stomach. The image of two big-bellied men physically shoving each other with their stomachs, fingers pointing at each other—power, intimidation. Excess!

If you learn to clean out your energy field you do not have to be at the beck and call of outside forces. You no longer need to react to those people who attempt to control you in any form. When the energy is blocked, you may want to go off and belt them, break down in tears, or hold it inside and seethe until you explode. By de-energizing the energy, the emotions, you regain control of your life, yourself. You can be so secure within yourself, so at peace, so centered, that what a person says, or what happens around you, does not control your behavior or reactions. You can always come back to the place of neutrality, amusement, and clear choice. A healthy, balanced, fully-functioning 3rd chakra creates a feeling of peace and inner harmony with your Self, life in general, and your place in life. You can accept yourself, your feelings, your experiences and also respect the feelings and character traits of others. Remember there's a great deal of joy, light, and love inside every one of us!

4th Chakra
HEART CHAKRA

The Heart Chakra! What a beautiful, beautiful chakra! The heart chakra is the center of the entire chakra system. It is the bridge between the lower three physical and emotional centers and the higher three mental and spiritual centers. This is where the best of both "worlds" integrate, facilitating the healing and transformation of yourself and others. As the heart chakra opens, so does your ability to connect with your Higher Power. The heart chakra radiates loving and forgiveness—where you develop the capacity to love. When you are open to receiving that love, you are then open to receiving the guidance from your higher wisdom. Open to the "wisdom of the heart."

Keep running energy, visualizing the beautiful, cleansing gold energy, dissolving issues as they come up. The color therapy for this chakra is pink and/or green, so you may find it helpful to breathe in those colors. Profound healings can take place in this chakra, so again, please be gentle with yourself, filling yourself with lots of compassion, forgiveness and amusement!

Take a look at yourself and your heart chakra. Some peoples' heart chakras are so big that they take in the whole community, and would nurture the universe if they could. Now, in theory, this is very lovely; however, practically speaking this will create a major energy drain. Are you someone who is always nurturing, mothering, listening to other's problems, taking care of others before you take care of yourself? Your kitchen (work station, office) usually full of people, talking with you, seeking your advice. You're the one who takes in stray cats and dogs—and sometimes people? You can usually recognize this type of person by the large chest, large bosom—a symbol of love, sustenance and nurturance. Remember: no judgments, no "rights" or "wrongs"—just awareness.

Who are you? How do you view yourself? The heart chakra is also connected with your sense of identity. If you've been exploring your chakras and thus raising your awareness of your beliefs and programming, running energy and dissolving issues as they come up, it's a pretty safe bet to say your concept of yourself is shifting. Healing and identity change takes place predominantly in the heart chakra. What are any images, concepts you may hold about who you think you *should* be? Who gave those to you? Who told you that you had to be that successful business person? Who told you that you only counted if you had high academic achievement? Who told you that you couldn't follow your heart's desire, that it was foolish and not a valid choice? What messages did you receive? Who broke your heart? Now's the time you can release the pain and the hurt, and fill your heart with forgiveness and love, knowing that you are divinely protected. Who was the first one to teach you that sometimes you can't trust? Who betrayed you? As children, we have wonderful, open hearts—you can see it. Children have an incredible joy of life, they are totally present. The heart is wide open, they haven't received any invalidation. You have the ability to achieve that again! What was the first incident where you learned it wasn't safe to be open? You don't have to remember it, but if an image comes in, dissolve it— no need to analyze. Did you experience betrayal, hurts, disappointments, loss? The loss of a beloved pet—pets are still family, especially to a child. Who left you? Siblings, parents, best friends? Did they die, move away, or leave you without warning? Did you hold on to the grief, the fear of losing? Did you develop a fear of intimacy, of getting close, and loving again— truly, truly loving? We've probably all done this or experienced this happening to us: allowing someone to get just "so close," and then pushing them back, because we didn't want to be vulnerable. We were afraid of losing—losing our identity, our hearts, ourselves.

When in your life have you closed down your heart chakra? Who in your life—be it family, co-worker or friend, comes from a place of coldness, stoicism and doesn't allow feelings and emotional expression? Who has the philosophy of "I won't let anyone get close enough to hurt me. I'm not willing to be vulnerable. I'm not willing to risk that." Is there any of that programming inside of you? If so, don't judge it, just release it, dissolve it, and *forgive yourself*. Forgiveness is associated with the heart chakra—forgiveness of yourself, the judgments you've placed upon yourself or another, forgiveness of others, and Divine forgiveness. It may not be possible at this stage of healing to truly forgive someone else's transgression. That's okay, don't force it. What's most important is that you forgive yourself and know that you are divinely loved.

Who have you allowed to create your identity for you? Teachers? Parents? Friends? Co-workers? Be aware that as you change, your identity, your sense of self, is also going to change. People may have to come and go from your life because of their inability to accept the change. They may invalidate the "you" that is emerging. They have a vested interest in the "old you." Let them go, and surround yourself with those who truly support you in being you! Who validates you? Who invalidates you? You can feel invalidation in your heart, usually as a tenseness in the back—a sadness, a darkness. If the heart chakra is not balanced, you can turn into a people-pleaser, seeking approval because of a desperate need for outside validation. Take a moment now and give yourself validation. Visualize a beautiful pink or green ball of validation and breathe that into your heart chakra, filling yourself up with that love, self-love and compassion.

At any time in your life have you suffered from asthma? Bronchitis? Pneumonia? Heart problems? These are heart chakra-related health conditions. When someone develops asthma, oftentimes it's from feeling smothered—"smother love"—feeling weight on your chest, your heart, as if someone is sitting on you. Release that now. The 2nd and 4th chakras have a unique interrelationship. The uterus (in the 2nd) is sometimes referred to as the "low heart" while the heart in the chest is referred to as the "high heart." If a woman's low heart (2nd chakra) has been blocked through rape, incest, or abuse, a woman cannot truly open her high heart until the healing process has started in the low heart. In our culture, women also tend to shut down their low hearts (sexuality and erotic needs) because we're taught that "nice girls aren't sexual." Yet we're also taught that it is okay to be in touch with our emotions and feelings through the heart chakra—so there is a set up for conflict between the 2nd and 4th chakras.

According to Dr. Christiane Northrup, studies have shown personality differences between patients with cervical cancer (2nd chakra) and breast or lung cancer (4th chakra). One study showed that 50 percent of the cervical cancer patients had physically lost their fathers due to death or desertion during childhood. Typically, these patients show other 2nd-chakra related traits: multiple marriages, high incidence of sexual activity with partners they neither loved nor respected, over concern with body shape and size, and also a feeling of being neglected as children. In contrast, in the homes of those with breast cancer (4th chakra-related illness), the father was *emotionally* distant (a 4th chakra-related pattern). These patients had a greater tendency to stay in a loveless marriage, a relatively high likelihood of carrying a heavy load of responsibility for younger siblings during childhood, and a greater chance of denying themselves medical care and physical nurturance.

Take a moment and notice who's corded you in your heart chakra. Usually cords in the heart chakra mean, "I like you," or "I love you." There can also be some cords in there that may be conditional, "I'll like you IF. . . , I'll love you IF. . . , I'll approve of you IF. . ." If you feel any cords, remove them gently, you don't have to tear anything out. Sometimes, it's okay to leave some of the cords in there. There may be someone you love who just corded you to say "hi." Maybe you'd like to keep that one in there for a little while and take it out later—holding that someone close to your heart is fine. Generally speaking, you don't want too many cords because then you would not be running on your own energy, but on other people's, thus living with their beliefs, conditions, etc. If the cord is not draining you of energy, then it's not too harmful. We don't have to be "cord-free." If we were "cord-free," we couldn't operate in a loving way, connecting with fellow beings or experiencing the oneness with life. Where do you think the concept of "heart strings" came from? They are literally little cords from the heart chakra that were sent out for love. Check to see who you've corded from the heart. See if you want to call your energy back to you and give it back to yourself. Who have you been seeking approval from? Who have you been wanting love from? When affection is not equally reciprocated, it can be painful. That's when it's time to pull those heartstrings back. Reclaim you own energy. Fill your heart with your own love, compassion, and approval.

Parents and spouses love to cord the heart chakra because it can be disguised and enters the chakra as "love." Sometimes there's a little tricky cord that'll go through the heart and sneak down into the 3rd, and voila, you have *conditional* love. "I love you—but I want to control you. If you do this, I'll love you—"

Any beliefs about being "spiritual" with a loving, open heart and NO BOUNDARIES? Nip that one in the bud! Being loving and compassionate to yourself means setting boundaries for yourself, giving yourself the capacity to love. Operating from the heart chakra doesn't mean you have to be lovey-dovey all the time, or that you go around in a big, glommy group hugging each other and you never separate! That's not what "coming from the heart" is about. That happens sometimes, but when you feel it, make separations. You'll know if you're corded, because you'll be thinking about that person or group almost obsessively, and your ability to be clear will be affected. Once again, set boundaries! Loving does not mean being a doormat! Loving is loving yourself enough to be very clear on what you will tolerate in your life, what you won't and what you will welcome into your space.

The heart chakra is a powerful healer. When you have opened your heart, a mere look, a mere thought can assist in healing someone else as well as yourself. The heart is essential in counseling (heart-centered listening), healing, and transformation. It's a good idea to keep it clean, however. Make separations the moment you start feeling heavy in the heart. You can still be loving and not have them living in your heart chakra. You'll be able to love them better and be a more effective counselor.

We hide a lot of issues in the back of our chakras, particularly the heart chakra. That's where we carry childhood fears, invalidation, and hurts. So just now, visualize a river of pink, green, or gold energy gently flowing through the chakra, releasing any energy that has been stuck and that you're willing and ready to let go. Just let it flow out, let it release. Fill yourself up with you own loving: unconditional love, acceptance and forgiveness. As you're doing this, if there are images of people or situations, you may want to visualize and place them in a beautiful, pink rose or pink bubble, so that you no longer have to carry the resentment or the hurt. Just go ahead and place them in there for forgiveness. Let them receive the blessings. Release the bubble into the highest realms. Now you can release yourself from those restrictions and receive the blessings.

With an open heart chakra, your creativity flows because you've opened to more of the childlike qualities of innocence, joy, and freedom. Your natural healing abilities also awaken—you may notice your touch containing more healing energy. You may feel heat emanating from your hands. That's healing energy flowing from the back of the heart chakra, down the arm channels and out the palms of the hands. With guidance and practice, that energy can be used for assisting others in their healing. Massage therapists, body workers, and spiritual healers all incorporate this healing energy into their work.

While we're exploring the heart chakra, you may want to ask for clarification regarding your "heart's desire." While breathing in the pink/green/gold energy, envision your Higher Self coming toward you, bringing you a gift. Receive this gift. You are worthy to receive. This gift can assist you in achieving and/or clarifying your heart's desire. Maybe it's a tool you can use, or perhaps inspiration, or kind loving words. Validation. You always have access to this gift. With an open, balanced heart chakra, you have access to your Higher Power, divine love, inspiration and forgiveness at any time. I encourage you to listen to and follow the wisdom of your heart.

5th Chakra
THROAT CHAKRA

This is the chakra that keeps AT&T in business—"Your true voice"! The throat chakra relates to communication, personal expression, and speaking your truth! Located at the base of the larynx, the 5th chakra is also the energy center through which you receive your "inner voice" and inner guidance by developing your clairaudient (clear hearing) abilities. Some of the dysfunctions associated with this chakra include chronic sore throats, throat and mouth ulcers, gum disease, temporo-mandibular joint disease (TMJ), scoliosis, thyroid disease, swollen glands, laryngitis and stuttering. Have you ever experienced any of these conditions? Perhaps someone in your family has?

As we explore the 5th chakra, I once again urge you to take care of yourself. Keeping a glass of water handy while exploring this chakra might be useful, as sometimes the throat may dry and tense up as the issues come forward during this exploration. Also, breathing in a light, clear shade of sky blue creates calmness, and can soothe and clear the throat chakra. As always, forgive yourself if any judgments surface and fill yourself with love and compassion.

How comfortable are you about speaking your truth? Are there fears associated with it? We learned at an early age that it wasn't safe to speak up. "Children should be seen and not heard. If you can't say anything nice, don't say anything at all." Were you ever slapped for speaking up? So you learned not to. Become aware of the programs available about speaking what you truly feel, expressing what you believe to be true. Sometimes the fear is based on survival—the belief that you might perish if you speak up. Especially if what you have to say is not presently popular or may be perceived as threatening to a certain structure. Think of all the innocent women and men who were burned at the stake or hanged during the Salem witch trials, or people labeled as traitors if they spoke against the government. People were beaten or whipped for speaking out to the "boss." You can see how the fear of speaking up is a very real fear. It may not be a current fear, but such fears did exist at one time and have affected us. Fear is passed from generation to generation. We constantly receive messages to keep quiet. Keep dissolving the issues as they come up. In relationships, do you avoid the truth out of fear that your partner will leave? Have you experienced that? You do not have to be run by your fear pictures. You can release that fear, dissolve the issues. You are safe to speak your truth: that's what you're here to do.

What about the image of being on a soapbox? Speaking your truth does not necessarily mean you are "on your soapbox," trying to cram words, ideas, or thoughts down somebody's throat. That's not speaking "truth" as much as it is defending a point of view shrouded with uncertainty. How much has been crammed down your throat? There's probably been a lot through the years— words that were "hard to swallow." What beliefs have been crammed down there? It's okay to let them up, let them out, and release them.

As children we thought that words were very powerful, that they may even have the power to kill. If we were to say anything perceived as mean or ungrateful, we got the impression that it would kill the person we said it to. It could have been a statement as innocent as: "That really hurts me to hear you say that. It kills me." That's all it takes to get the message across. "Don't say anything to hurt anyone or they might die." Words may hurt, but they certainly don't kill. Somebody may not want to hear what you have to say, but that does not take away your right to say it. You may have learned to temper your expression in order to not rock the boat and keep peace at all costs.

We're talking about free expression, expressing who we truly are. Do you feel nervous when you're about to speak something that is very true and very dear to your heart? The 5th chakra is the bridge between the heart and the mind, providing the ability to put what's in your heart or mind into words to be expressed to the world through the throat. If the energy is blocked, one or both of the following may happen: either you find it difficult to reflect about your feelings and therefore express your unresolved emotions in thoughtless actions. Or else you may shut yourself off inside your intellect, and deny your emotions a right to live. The only feelings you permit are the ones that have passed through the filter of your self-judgment and which do not contradict the judgment of the people around you.

What is your voice like? Are you afraid of being heard? Is your voice soft, barely audible so that people are always asking you to speak louder, to enunciate? Maybe you were afraid you would never be heard, so you developed a loud, brash voice. Is it shrill or melodious? Think of people in your life, lawyers for example, who talk crisply and loudly, trying to overpower with their words and voice. That is a dysfunctional chakra, that is not free expression, or respecting another's free will.

What else did your parents tell you about speaking up? Maybe they didn't *say* anything, but they sent you mixed messages? Did you sense or feel one "truth" and yet get invalidated as they spoke another? This chakra is about clear, honest communication. Not only with others but with yourself, with your inner wisdom, your Higher Power. Do you stutter when you get excited, when you're ready to say something that is very true for you? Do you suddenly become very shy, thinking that what you have to say isn't worth being heard, afraid of being rejected?

Are you artistic? Do you paint, draw, write, create poetry, but are afraid to share it with anyone? This has to do with creative expression, located in your 5th chakra. How okay is it with you to express your anger, or does your throat tighten up and the words not come out? How much permission do you have to speak what you truly feel? Or are you censoring it? This is a powerful, wonderful, wonderful chakra. It's our expression. It can be full of joy, upliftment, song—the freedom to sing, to express.

As you balance the throat chakra energy, you gain the clarity to communicate with the Higher Self—to hear its guidance. This is because your auditory senses (hearing) and the throat chakra are located in the same area. Are there certain things you don't want to hear, so you just don't hear them? Do you have selective hearing? As a child, did you suffer from earaches? Was there anger in the household that you didn't want to hear, so you blocked it out, creating ear problems? Take a moment and imagine golden Q-Tips. Now energetically clean out your ears—your clairaudient channels. Your ears may even pop as you visualize the golden Q-Tips cleaning out your ears. Do you experience throat problems? When you are tired, is your throat the most vulnerable to stress? Strep Throat? Raspy throat? Having to "cough up" what you need to say to release what is in your heart? When you do finally have the courage to express your anger, do you punish yourself? Does your throat start hurting? Do you wind up sick the next day? Just things to be aware of. Again, no judgments. There are no "rights" or "wrongs." The only way of healing is through love—loving yourself, forgiving yourself, and forgiving others who may have jammed unwanted programming down your throat.

Do you place a lot of emphasis on words? Verbal wit—are you able to "slice" with your words? Do you have to find the perfect word, rather than allowing yourself to speak spontaneously? I encourage you to release these issues. Now is the time to fill yourself with love and forgiveness, and to release any judgments you may have for not speaking up or perhaps for saying too much—whatever the judgment may be. Forgive yourself for the time(s) you didn't say, "I love you," when you wanted to. You were afraid, afraid of rejection. Release the fear. You are responsible only for communicating. You're not responsible for someone else's "getting it." Sometimes they just can't "get it." Sometimes they can and will, but you're not responsible for making sure they do. Release those responsibility issues: "Oh, if I just would have communicated a bit clearer, then this never would have happened." When you know you've done the best you can, it's best to let go of the need for the other person to completely understand your message. Let yourself off the hook.

Check and see if there are any cords in this chakra. Sometimes, as you're speaking to people, particularly salespeople, they will cord you in the 5th—to hold your attention while they deliver the sales pitch. They want to tell you what to say. (Say "yes.") Bosses may also do that. If you're "representing" the company, they want to make sure you present the "correct, appropriate" image. No one has a right to control what you say and how to say it, robbing you of your honest expression. When someone is thinking of you, he or she will sometimes throw energy into your 5th chakra as if to say: "I want to talk with you. I want to communicate with you. Call me." That's fine, but you still may want to remove the cord, because if it's a big one, or if there are a number of them, it will create a sore throat. If you do a lot of talking on the phone, it's a good idea to regularly balance and clear out this chakra. Have you ever leaned forward, straining to listen to a person (throwing your energy on them) rather than relying on yourself to relax, sit back, and listen.   Or perhaps you've experienced the sensation of talking in a group and suddenly being overcome with a tickle in the throat, coughing, etc. Probably somebody threw their energy on you to try to hear you!

The throat center is also associated with nourishment. It indicates your ability to receive the nourishment of life. Are you able to receive; are you able to take it in? Can you freely and clearly communicate your needs? If not, who put a lid on it? We all have our own "song to sing." Do you like your singing voice? Do you think you can't sing? Let go of any issues about the quality of your voice, and whether it's "not good enough," or you've been praised for it constantly. Release any "perfect" pictures about singing or speaking properly, of doing it "right." Do you have issues about proper diction? Do you have an accent? We all have accents, it just depends who you're talking to. Where do you place your voice? Back of the throat, roof of the mouth, behind the nose creating a nasal quality? Do you allow your voice to resonate at its perfect pitch? Sound facilitates healing. Your voice can heal. You don't have to say anything profound, so release those "performance issues." It is the quality of your voice, the sound vibration, that heals and soothes or excites and motivates. Love your voice. You have a beautiful voice. Let it be heard. Speak kind words to yourself! You deserve them! Fill yourself with confidence! Freedom of expression! Trust in your freedom to speak your truth with confidence!

6th Chakra
THIRD EYE

Welcome to the 6th chakra, the brow chakra, otherwise referred to as the "third eye." This energy center is located in the center of the forehead between the eyebrows and is associated with clairvoyance (clear seeing), higher mental wisdom, personal vision, visualization, intuition, imagination, and insight. This chakra can also influence how you see yourself in the world, how others perceive you, or how you think they perceive you.

So go ahead and start dissolving any issues that may be surfacing already. Visualize a beautiful transparent indigo blue color that you can breathe into the chakra. Remember to be kind to yourself as you take a look at some of the issues associated with the 6th chakra. View the issues from a place of amusement when possible; bring in love, compassion, and barrels of forgiveness. Ask to release any blockages that can be released at this time, for the highest good, and create a safe space around you.

How much permission do you have to see things clearly? Do you have a filter over your eyes? Do you experience any eyesight challenges? Those of you who wear contacts or glasses might want to take a look at what age you decided you no longer wanted to see things clearly. When did you need to change your perception, to make things more soft focus. What were the events leading up to it? Did you alter your perception when you entered puberty? What was your attitude about your glasses? Proud? Embarrassed? Confused? Something to hide behind? Were you amazed at the visual clarity? (That there were actually individual leaves on the trees?) Clarity. That quality has a lot to do with the functioning of the 6th chakra. When the 6th chakra is cleaned out, running harmoniously, you'll see things very clearly. You know what direction to follow. You follow your inner guidance. You have a bird's-eye view.

Do you regard high mental capabilities, scholastic achievements, intellect, or science in higher esteem than intuition? Or perhaps there was someone in your family who did and who discredited your intuition? The 6th chakra is also about tapping into your higher mental capabilities, higher knowledge and wisdom. Yet, if that chakra is not balanced, you can become an "intellectual snob" and look down upon anyone who does not have an academic degree or who operates primarily from intuition and feeling instead of intellect. Have you bought into any of those beliefs regarding the intellect being superior to intuition? What about those in your family or your surroundings? Are you dealing with a bunch of intellectual snobs? Keep dissolving pictures of anyone who was coming from that position who invalidated you. Realize that it's possible to achieve a wonderful balance of philosophy, science, and intuition. They can work harmoniously together, complementing each other.

What's you personal history with headaches? Do you get a lot of them? This may stem from an imbalance in the 6th chakra. Maybe you're trying to "see too hard"; scrunching up your face and your brow, forcing all the energy to the front of your face, which oftentimes creates a tension headache. You can exert this kind of effort when you're "planning for the future," strategizing, or anticipating the results of your actions. How are your sinuses? Do you have problems with allergies, with your sinuses? When you start feeling blockages in your nasal passages, dissolve any issues or situations that you may have recently experienced and visualize gold energy flowing through the passages. This is all connected with the 6th chakra. Do you hold tension in your head, behind your eyes? Take a moment to relax, relax your eyes, allowing that color to come in—the gold—bathe in it, relax, and keep dissolving those pictures. Other dysfunctions related to this chakra include brain tumors, blood clots, neurological disorders, blindness, deafness, spinal difficulties, seizures, learning disabilities, lack of concentration, mental confusion, and lack of spiritual understanding or vision.

Mental stability is also associated with the 6th chakra. "Crazy" pictures—insanity. It has been noted that some people whose chakras are not balanced, not functioning properly, may have the ability to see "visions." But if their grounding is not secure, they will not be able to incorporate those visions into reality, so they do not have a sense of reality, and go off in a fantasy world of their own. They do not know how to function in reality. There is a fine line between genius and insanity.

You, yourself, may not have those fears about yourself, but check your family. Does anyone, even jokingly say, "Oh you're crazy for doing or thinking that"? What part of you believed that? What part of you, as you develop more of these intuitive skills and share your experiences with people in the mainstream, feels judged? Do they send you crazy pictures, like you're "really out there"? "You're in L.A., the land of the fruits and nuts." Dissolve those pictures.

What about any issues regarding witchcraft, magic, white magic, or black magic? Do you experience fear at the mention of those ideas? When the chakra is imbalanced a person may attempt to use the power of the mind to manipulate others—yet this action is coming from a place of will power, not from a pure place in accordance with the highest good. This is where the term "black magic" comes in: manipulating someone, willing something on someone, or willing something to happen, controlling for personal advancement and gain, casting spells and magic. This covers only the potentially "negative" aspects of the power of the mind. There are also extremely positive ways to utilize this energy, which we'll cover a little bit later. However, people who try to manipulate others are not often "magicians," but are regular people who have chakras that are out of balance.

The 6th chakra is also the center of telepathy, the center from which you can send thoughts, images, and visualizations to another person. This is commonly referred to as mental telepathy. Do you have fears, doubts, beliefs, or disbeliefs about psychic abilities, clairvoyance, ESP—especially about developing your own abilities? What about "past lives"? Do you think you have lived before? If so, what past lives come up for you? Lifetimes of misusing your power? Perhaps experiencing someone else misusing power, and your life being affected by it? Have any religious convictions been placed upon you insinuating that developing this chakra is evil? Who told you that? Was it an organization? A teacher? A religion? A parent? Release any fears about misusing your abilities. It is your God-given right, your innate gift, to be able to see clearly and to function clearly: to use your higher mental powers and intuition as tools. As you open this center to a greater degree and balance it, you'll be able to tap into your higher wisdom and recognize the interconnectedness of the universe.

Do you sense any cords in your 6th chakra? A cord in your 6th chakra indicates that someone is "in your head." That is a major no-no! No one should be in your head except you. If someone else's energy is there, this person may be mentally trying to control or manipulate you, to get you to do what he or she wants you to do (mind games). Absolutely remove that cord and send the energy back to where it came from. If someone has corded you in the 6th, you may experience a headache. Someone may just be thinking of you intensely, wondering what you're up to and "jump into your head." Even if the intention is harmless, it's still best to remove the cord and reclaim your own energy!

Do you see yourself as a creative person? How easy is it for you to visualize, use mental imagery? Can you visualize? Do you give yourself permission to use your imagination? Do you recognize the power of imagination? Do you operate primarily from a mental place of logic and reason? Maybe it's affecting different areas of your life. In some situations you do want to utilize your ability to see clearly and use your intuition. In other circumstances, it's necessary to use logic and rationale, but the trick is, *balance*. We've all seen people who are out of balance and project one extreme or the other. Extreme mental focus can literally be seen in the brow area—protruding, overdeveloped eyebrows. There's a heaviness about them, an inability to relate on any level except mental and logical.

Do you recall incidents when you've "lost your head"? Perhaps this happened in a situation where you became confused and allowed yourself to get ungrounded, which affects your 6th chakra and your ability to be clear. This is an example of the interrelationship of the chakras—for they function best when in alignment with each other. When one chakra is blocked, it affects the other energy centers. Someone who is "spaced out," confused, and scattered is probably operating with a dysfunctional 6th chakra and lack of grounding (1st chakra) at that time.

Double check the front of your brow—do you feel pressure? Has someone put his or her hand (energetically speaking) over your third eye? Does he or she not want you to "see"? What shouldn't you see? Remove that "hand" and send the energy away. Parents will do that; so will employers or acquaintances, because they don't want you to see what's truly going on. Often when you see what the "truth" is and dare to speak it, you are invalidated, and so is everyone who does it. You do it to yourself! When was the last time you covered your eyes because you didn't like what you were seeing? Well, you can do the same thing on an energy level. This sometimes happens in counseling sessions when you get too close to uncovering a truth. Suddenly you feel a pain in the head—which in essence "blinds" you.

How do you see yourself? Take a really good look. Is that truly how you see yourself? Or is the image one of how others perceive you? If there's a discrepancy between the way you view yourself and the way others view you, you may want to check it out. Again, no judgments—just release. Let go and forgive. Can you see yourself as successful, whole, and complete? Do you see yourself as needy? Insufficient? What you see, what you focus on and visualize is what you get. Form follows thought! This chakra is a center for manifestation: where we can create our dreams and turn them into reality. So, if you visualize yourself as successful, happy, joy-filled, abundant, that's what you can create. It can be challenging when you are surrounded by negativity.

However, if you focus on what doesn't work and on the negative, that is what you'll create. This is where the adage, "you can't afford the luxury of a negative thought," comes in. This can also affect your health: Do you visualize yourself healthy? Do you put time restraints on your visualizations? Do you say, "Oh, in the future," "Later." You can declare it for NOW! "I am happy, healthy, abundant, joy-filled and loved NOW!" It's okay to visualize what you want. You have to be able to see it before you can create it. Seeing doesn't necessarily mean physically "seeing it" with your eyes: it may be sensing it, feeling it in the body, knowing it on an instinctual level. Creative visualization is very powerful, effective and a lot of fun! And as always, when you visualize, always ask "for the highest good." Sometimes you may want something, but if you manifest it in the physical, it might not be for your highest good. Or you may get what you asked for, but it may look different than you imagined it would. Your Higher Power knows what's truly for your highest good!

Dare to dream! Reach for the stars! Actually this is what the nature therapy for this chakra is. Visualize a beautiful dark starry night, gazing upon the stars, getting lost in their expansiveness and totality, the beauty of nature. It's awe-inspiring. Feel the wonder of it, even though the immensity may be far beyond your ability at the moment to possibly understand. But it's all there—all the information, all the loving, all the abundance. Just open yourself to receive it, recognize it. Breathe that beautiful indigo blue in, feel it flowing through the chakra, back and forth, cleansing, letting it purify, the beautiful blue ray.

An open third eye assists you with embracing a holistic approach, a holistic vision; not just scientific, academic, or intuitive feeling, but the whole picture; the expansiveness, the ability to see beyond the emotion, to see beyond the intellect. You are free to see whatever you choose to see, whatever you want to see. Really own that. Know that. You have clear eyes.

7th Chakra
CROWN CHAKRA

The 7th chakra—the crown chakra—is located at the top of the head. This center is associated with your free will; the highest knowingness, divinity, consciousness. Without the 7th chakra being opened, none of the other chakras can come into balance. The 7th chakra is the first chakra to develop in an infant—the last one being the 1st chakra, when the infant is born into the physical world. Through the 7th, we get our divine inspiration, divine creativity. This is the visionary center. This is the chakra where everything comes together; where the information from all chakras integrates. Things that maybe made sense individually now come together so you can form the totality of the concept, the total picture. This is your pure intuition. Purity.

Be sure to stay in the center of your head and stay grounded as much as possible. Breathe in a beautiful violet color, perhaps even clear white and gold. When your 7th chakra is open and balanced, there's peace, serenity, knowingness and connection with all.

You may want to check your 7th chakra for any cords of energy. Cords in this chakra are a big taboo, as they indicate that an attempt is being made to control your free will. Some religions, gurus, spiritual organizations, and corporations attempt to take away a person's individual free will or free choice. You've witnessed the glassy-eyed "devotees" who don't think for themselves anymore, but who are part of a total group mind. They don't know how to make decisions, have given away their power, don't own their body and aren't really even aware of their body. The 7th chakra is concerned with ownership of your body. Sometimes spiritual teachers will place a small cord in the crown while the student is studying with them, to assist in "feeding the information." That may not be great, yet if the cord is removed after the information has been transferred, then it's harmless. Some of the more unsavory "gurus" may leave the cord in to insure that you "follow their teachings." These are the gurus or religious leaders who believe that their teachings are the "only right ones." Religious fanatics operate in this manner, whether it's Christianity, Mormon, Catholicism, Judaism, Hare Krishna, Scientology, Buddhism, etc., there are usually some "fanatics" who get carried away and want to recruit the whole world. Any organized religion that takes away your ability to think for yourself, that takes away the concept that you have the right to direct communication with the Creator, to God, to Buddha, the Supreme Being (whatever name you want to place on it), is an organization that may not be good for you. There is a difference between religion and spirituality. Does any anger and resentment come up for you? Dissolve it. Release it and bring in forgiveness!

Have you experienced anyone in your life who has intimidated you, brought up fear, and tried to control you through the belief that if you do this or that, then God won't love you? You're going to Hell. You're a sinner, not worthy of God's love. Take a look at those beliefs. The patriarchal dominance of the church—the control. Are you aware of any anger, righteousness, or fear about being suppressed? Those were people operating from a dysfunctional 7th chakra. They try to squash people's 7th chakras, to control, to take away free will to preserve the reign of church or state, to maintain control over the masses. That's not what spirituality is about these days. What about the Goddess religion? Dissolve any pictures of oppression that may come up. It's okay to be reminded of the oppression of personal or spiritual rights—to remind you of the anger, hurt and betrayal as long as it propels you into being more determined to be conscious and aware and not to let those emotions run you. That's not the lesson this lifetime. Free will is your inherent birthright!

It's not just spiritual organizations—corporations will try to cord your crown sometimes. They encourage the group mind so you'll work and live for the "good of the company." Fanaticism happens, too. Look at some of the pictures that may come up about the military, the militia, pro-choice groups, pro-life groups, gay rights activists, feminists. Keep dissolving the issues as they come up. Know and trust that this lifetime is about free will and free choice for yourself, your own connection to the Divine, and your right to have that connection.

Take a look at some of the artists. Look at their creative blocks. Maybe they are not allowing Spirit to work through them. Think about your lack of inspiration. A lack of divine inspiration is one of the qualities of a dysfunctional 7th chakra. Confusion is the inability to make decisions because someone else is trying to tell you what to do. In severe cases, people will contract fatal diseases and illnesses if they've been resistant to and negligent toward their spiritual path. Sometimes they'll get an illness to slow them down, give them time to reflect upon their lives, to find values, to go beyond the physical and material world in search of something greater. Often it's a big wake-up call, asking that person, inviting that person to go further, reach higher, release the lower attachment, come higher and raise their vibrations. Now's the time.

Sometimes brain problems have to do with a shut-down in the 7th. Dissolve any pictures that may be coming up regarding unworthiness to be connected with the Divine. You are already operating on very lovely, high vibrations, or you wouldn't be reading this, and doing this work. Remind yourself of your worthiness to have serenity, to receive divine guidance and feel the total connection.

Do you have any beliefs about spirituality and what it means to be a "spiritual" person? "Spirituality means you have to be nice all the time.

One can't be angry and be spiritual." Do you have any beliefs about the food you eat and your spirituality? "You can't eat onions or garlic and be spiritual. You can't eat meat and have high vibrations. You must eat this, you must do that." Just take a look at some of the beliefs. Some may be perfectly valid for you, but you don't have to buy into anyone else's beliefs of what has worked for them, or the beliefs from various nutritional gurus. What are your beliefs about being a spiritual being? Smiling all the time? Does being spiritual mean you're floating, ungrounded? Do you have any beliefs about being in your body, or that if you are in your body you are not spiritual? That you're being punished for being in your body? That there are limitations, restrictions? Some of your beliefs may be very, very subtle, beliefs that you were just handed as a child, or absorbed over time. Just see if you bought into anything, as to what your spirituality is to you. Are there people around you who believe you have to practice a certain doctrine? That you have to practice a certain method to be spiritual, to be connected? Do you have permission to disagree?

Your spirituality, your path is yours. It's whatever works for you. It may not work for Joe Blow on the street or anyone else, but it's valid if it works for you. We've not been supported in that, growing up. We have been supported and encouraged to always conform, to belong to a group. Certainly it's fine to be in a group, if it works for you! Always remember what works for you may not work for someone else. Don't cram your beliefs down their throats or bonk them in their 7th! Remember the image of the "fire and brimstone" preachers pounding on the pulpit— attempting to pound their beliefs into your head, into your crown! Let that image go!

Sound therapy for the 7th chakra is silence. Take a moment and feel the silence, feel the connection of your Divinity, the highest knowledge, serenity and peace. Imagine that you are alone at the top of a mountain, where you can see it all. Everything is clear to you. There are no distractions, just peace, silence, serenity on the highest mountain peak, the highest you can get to the Source, to God. Be open to the miracles that happen every day. That's the gift, the opportunity, of a balanced 7th chakra.

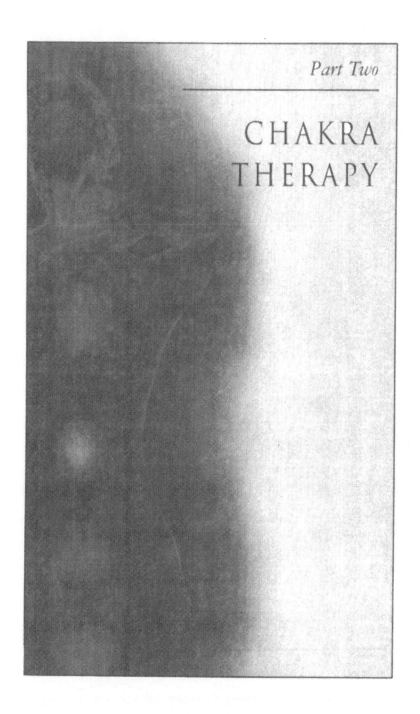

Part Two

CHAKRA
THERAPY

Basic Skills
for Clearing Your
Energy Field

In the previous section you explored the psychological and physical effects of blocked energy and how it can drastically alter your beliefs, health, well-being, and ability to function in the world. In this section, you will learn some basic techniques for clearing your energy field, releasing "stuck" energy, and restoring your natural state of harmony and neutrality.

Grounding

I've referred to the word "grounding" numerous times throughout this book, and now I'd like to explain to you what is meant by this term. Using the concept of a ship, "grounding" is similar to the act of dropping an anchor. A ship floats aimlessly, vulnerable to the effect of its surroundings until it is safely anchored. Once anchored, the ship is relatively steady and secure, safely mobile, until the anchor is reeled in. Using this concept, you are the ship and "grounding" is what anchors you to this planet. Grounding provides your body a firm foundation or connection to the Earth, creating a sense of physical security, focus, and ability to manifest on the physical planet. Like most people you probably like having what you want on this planet (new car, money, house, relationships) and in order to be more effective in your ability to create this for yourself, you need to be connected to this planet. Otherwise what you want to create remains just a great idea, or a wish, floating out there in another realm with no way of manifesting in your physical reality. On a spiritual level, grounding provides the means to keep your Spiritual Being in touch with its physical manifestation, your body. As above, so below. As contradictory as it may seem, you really do need your body to live a spiritual life. Spirit needs a vehicle in order to manifest on this planet, and that vehicle needs to be connected to Earth in order to channel the higher spiritual information from above to Earth below. If you're not grounded, your energy leaves your body and leaves your body vulnerable to harm. It's a privilege to have a body, so take care of it by respecting and honoring your physical being as well as your spiritual being.

Grounding is not an event that happens once and suddenly you're grounded for life. Chances are you will lose your grounding many times, probably more times than you have it at first because of stressful situations around you. Any time you perceive you are in danger, or feeling threatened, your grounding disappears. Perhaps the boss is yelling at you, you're walking down an unfamiliar street, or there's an earthquake. It doesn't matter if the danger is real or not, if you perceive it as threatening, then in your reality it is, and you may lose your grounding when you need it the most. The trick is learning to recognize when you're not grounded, so you can ground again. When you feel spacey, your mind goes blank, it's difficult to put words together, you feel flushed, your heart races or you find it difficult to concentrate; you have probably lost your grounding. That happens sometimes. Just ground yourself again and keep going. How do you ground yourself? In the following section I'll share with you a grounding technique I use, and will define the terms "present time" and "center of your head," which are important to the grounding process, and then provide some additional grounding techniques.

A Grounding Technique

First, sit upright in a chair in an open body position. By "open body" I mean avoid crossing any part of your body, such as ankles, legs, arms, or

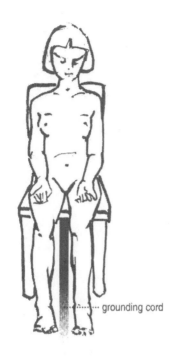

grounding cord

Figure 2. A grounding technique.

hands (see figure 2 on page 79). This position helps your body relax and encourages your energy to flow. Now, remove your shoes, and place your feet flat on the floor, or on a pillow on the floor, if your feet don't touch. Removing your shoes gives your feet the opportunity to relax as well as giving you a chance to make direct contact with the floor. Wearing socks is fine. It can be distracting and uncomfortable if your feet get cold.

As you sit comfortably, close your eyes, breathe normally, and become aware of your body. Feel the weight of your body against the chair. Let the chair support you as you focus your attention on your hips and the back of your legs against the chair. Feel your feet against the floor. Continue this body awareness process as you take nice deep breaths, inhaling and exhaling a minimum of three times, relaxing deeper with each breath.

For all these exercises, I will be asking you to use your imagination to visualize an image in your mind's eye or sense what I'm suggesting you do. As much as possible, don't think about it. Let it be effortless. If you can visualize, great. If visualizing an image is challenging to you, don't worry about it, because form follows thought. All you have to do is think it, and before the thought is complete, it's done on an energy level.

Now that you're relaxed and aware, imagine (visualize) a cord (or pole, string, rope, wire, chain, beam of light, tree or whatever appears in your mind's eye) of energy flowing from your 1st chakra (located at the base of your spine if you're a man, or between your ovaries if you're a

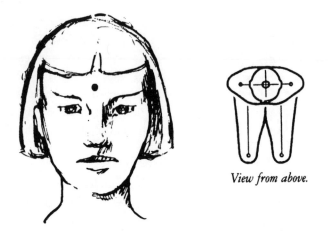

View from above.

Figure 3. Locate and stay in the center of your head, the neutral space that physically exists in your head.

woman) all the way into the deep center of the earth. This is your grounding cord. Attach your grounding cord to the center of the earth by whatever means you can think of: wrapping the cord around the earth's center, using a giant magnet, or dropping anchor and hooking it on the earth's center. Use your imagination. There are no rights or wrongs. But I do recommend that you make your grounding cord as big as you want. A tiny, whispery thin grounding cord isn't going to do much good in times of stress.

That's it! You're grounded! Take a moment to practice. Please note that your eyes do not have to be closed in order to ground, as a matter of fact it's probably better if they're open. We close our eyes during these exercises just to minimize external distractions to make it easier to concentrate. Now with eyes open or shut, visualize pulling your grounding cord up, notice any difference and then ground again. Repeat several times. This process helps you to realize that you are a powerful creator and that you do indeed have control over your energy. Do you feel any different? Often, my clients feel their legs for the first time. It can be a strange sensation if you're not used to it, but stay with it and enjoy. If you'd like to refine the technique and make your grounding more potent, try the following:

Visualize your grounding cord extending from the base of your spine and anchoring into the earth. Bring yourself into "present time." Focus only on the here and now, not letting your thoughts wander to events in the past or to possible future happenings. Stay in the present. You may be surprised to discover how challenging that can be at first, but keep practicing. Remember, the only way we can manifest on this physical planet is by being in the here and now! The past is done. We can learn from it, but we have to let it go. The future is ours to create right now, from being in the present time.

To strengthen your connection to the earth, you need to locate and stay in the center of your head. In order to accomplish this, imagine drawing a line ear to ear, right above the ears. Draw another line from the center of your brow to the back of your head. The place where the two lines intersect is the center of your head, a space that physically exists in your head (see figure 3, page 80). Think of this space as your control station, a neutral area directly behind your brow where you are safe and have the ability to view what's going on around you with com-passionate detachment, and without getting involved emotionally, men-tally, or physically.

Since this is your control center, it is important that no one else's energy occupy this space. It's not a great idea to have someone else con-trolling your thoughts or actions. So, take a moment and visualize the center of your head. Mentally check it out and see if you get a sense of anyone else in there. You may actually get an image of a person. If you do, just boot him or her out of the space and all the way outside of your aura. Take some time and clean out the center of your head, since it may have been some time since you've been there. I encourage you to visual-ize a broom sweeping away any cobwebs or dust. You can even imagine there's a trap door in the floor into which you can sweep the unwanted items. Imagine a chute from the trap door all the way into the earth, so that all the old energy is deposited in the earth to be transmuted and used for healing. When you are done, you can fill the center of your head with gold-colored energy to cleanse it. Now place yourself in the center of your head and claim it as your space. Remember, you are the only one who should be in the center of your head!

Although the above mentioned technique for grounding is quite sufficient in and of itself, there may be situations that call for additional methods to reconnect you with Earth and your body.

- When you know you are going into a potentially threatening situation (confrontation of any kind, an impending natural disaster, an important meeting) you may want to use triple grounding. Triple grounding is grounding from these three places: the base of your spine and from both of your feet. In addition to your regular grounding cord extending from the 1st chakra, visualize grounding cords extending from the bottom of your feet, from the arches where the foot chakras are located, and anchor all three grounding cords into the center of the earth. This gives you a very solid foundation and helps you own your space.

- One method of cleaning your chakras is to attach individual grounding cords to each chakra and to visualize any blocks or negativity draining away, down the grounding cord to the center of the earth. Then visualize gold energy to balance and stabilize the chakras. (This will be discussed further in the Balancing Energy portion of this section.)

When you feel light-headed, spacey, or emotionally, mentally, or physically drained, try one of the following techniques:

- Physical exercise: Take a brisk walk, do some jumping jacks, or dance. This breaks up any negativity and brings you back in touch with your body.

- Stand barefoot in the grass, or on the beach, to reconnect with Mother Earth. Let her energy flow up through your feet and fill you with vitality.

- Drink some water. It cleanses the system and renews the flow of energy.

- Take a shower or bath. Water is a wonderful cleanser and helps increase your body awareness.

- Have sex in the form of your choice. Sex validates the body and makes it real.

- Eat something. Food also validates the body.

Protection

Before proceeding to the Running Energy Meditation, I'd like to touch upon the subject of protection. When you practice the Running Energy Meditation you clear out your energy field, release negativity and hurt feelings, release a lot of old garbage and fill yourself with a positive, higher energy vibration. While you meditate you are in a more vulnerable state, and if you haven't shielded yourself from unwanted energy, you could inadvertently attract negative vibrations that don't belong in your energy field instead of attracting the positive, healing ones. Protection is simply surrounding yourself with a positive shield of energy so that no unwanted thought forms or entities can invade your space.

Protection Techniques

Based on my experience, I've found the best way to protect yourself is simply by asking for protection and being open to receive it. One of the ways I invoke protection is by sincerely requesting the following: "Just now, I ask to call myself forward into the light from the highest of highs, asking it to fill, surround and protect me for the highest good of all concerned. I also ask to be open to receiving your love, guidance and protection." Then trust that you are divinely protected.

If this seems an elusive concept to you, don't worry, there are other techniques. The following exercise may help to make the elusive concept of protection on an energy level more tangible. For this exercise you're going to use the image of a rose. The rose image represents a protective shield of energy. This rose or shield acts like a magnet, catching and absorbing the unwanted negative energy before it gets to you and disrupts your energy.

In order to provide full protection, it's a good idea to place a number of roses or shields in and around your energy field. Visualize big, beautiful roses outside of your aura—in front of you, behind you, to the right of you, to the left of you, above you and below you.

The fun, creative aspect about using the image of a rose as a shield is that you can periodically check on your rose and see how it's doing. If it's wilting, then you know it's been doing its job, so you can just replace it with another rose, of any color or shape. You can visualize anything as a shield, it doesn't have to be a rose. Use your imagination. We'll go over more transformational uses for the rose image in the Transforming Energy section.

If the rose technique doesn't resonate for you, or if you just want to try something else, here are some suggestions about how to protect yourself on an energy level.

Alternative Techniques

- One of the best protections is to remove your resistance. Be a "body of glass," letting energy flow through you without it meeting resistance and getting stuck.
- Pull your aura in closer toward your body by just suggesting it do so.
- Visualize clear white light filling, surrounding, and protecting you.
- Visualize a column of light extending from the highest of highs and anchoring into the center of the earth. Place yourself in that column of light.
- Burn sage or incense, or light candles to burn away negative energies.
- Visualize a gold protective crown on top of your head.
- Visualize a pyramid, breathe it around you and cover it with gold.
- Breathe in gold light and let it fill and surround you.
- Visualize mirrors around you, reflecting any negative energy back to its original source.
- Recite a prayer to invoke the assistance of saints and sages from throughout the ages, healing angels, etc. One of my favorite invocations is a prayer known as St. Patrick's Breastplate:

Christ Be With Me.
Christ Be Within Me.
Christ Before Me.
Christ Behind Me.
Christ On My Right Hand.

Christ On My left Hand.
Christ Above Me.
Christ Beneath Me.
Christ Round About Me.

(If you are uncomfortable with the word Christ, please sub-stitute the name of the Divine Being that resonates with your particular belief, i.e., Mother-Father, God, Goddess, Buddha, Shiva, Great Creator, Supreme Being.)

I encourage you to ask for protection at all times, not just when you're meditating. It's wonderful to experience the warmth, comfort, and secu-rity of the Divine protection that is rightfully yours.

Running Energy Meditation

So far you've learned how to connect with the planet, remain grounded for longer periods of time, and how to protect yourself from being affect-ed by negative energies. In this section you're going to learn a very pow-erful technique for clearing out your energy field, the Running Energy Meditation. It's like taking a wonderful energy shower that recharges your batteries and clears your thinking. A perfect antidote for the end of a stressful day, this meditation helps you rid yourself of other people's energies, gather your own energies that you've scattered throughout the day, and come to a place of balance and calm. On a psychological level, it assists with the healing and release of old patterns of beliefs, behaviors, and buried emotions by stirring up the energy and bringing issues to the surface so you can deal with them. The spiritual aspect of this medita-tion is that it helps raise the vibrational level of your energy field. The higher your vibrations, the clearer communication you have with your Higher Self, with the God Source, and the greater your ability is to heal. When you are in direct communication with the Divine Source you are a clearer channel for self-healing and the healing of others (teaching, counseling, whatever your path is).

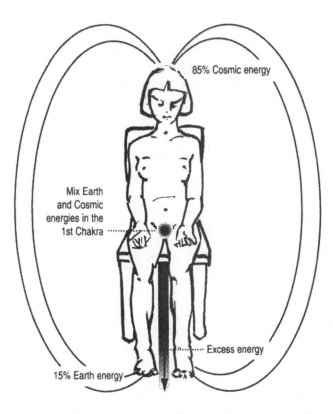

Figure 4. Running Energy Meditation. The excess energy goes down the grounding cord.

The Running Energy Meditation mixes the benevolent, nurturing, and healing energy of the earth with the higher vibration, spiritual, golden, cosmic energy of the universe. This meditation provides you with the proper balance of Earth and Cosmic energies, thus helping you maintain stability on all levels of existence (physical, emotional, mental, spiritual). From this balanced, stable, neutral state you can see clearly what needs to be done, make your own decisions, and generally, take control of your life.

First, you'll learn how to run Earth energy throughout your system. Next you'll learn how to run Cosmic energy throughout your system. Then, I'll explain to you step-by-step how to mix the two energies (Earth and Cosmic) together, and run the combined healing energies throughout your energy field.

As preparation for these exercises, sit in a chair, sitting up comfortably erect in an open body position, feet on the floor and eyes closed. As you may notice in figure 4, hands are relaxed, with palms facing upward. There are a number of other positions for your hands; for example, one palm facing up and the other facing down, or index fingers and thumbs on each hand touching, but for this exercise I recommend both palms facing up because it opens the hand chakras and allows the energy to flow in a simple, natural pattern. When the index finger and thumbs touch, the energy recirculates. One palm up represents energy directed upward, palm facing downward directs the energy toward the earth. All positions are valid, and feel free to experiment after you've practiced the techniques in the recommended way.

Step I: Running Earth Energy

- Visualize your grounding cord. Bring your awareness into the present time and locate the center of your head. (Please refer to the section on "Grounding" if you need a quick review.)
- Ask your feet and hand chakras to adjust to a size that is comfortable. Remember you don't have to think about it, the chakras know what size to adjust to.
- Imagine the light brown energy of Earth being drawn up through your
  > feet chakras;
  > calves;
  > knees;
  > lower and upper thighs;
  > 1st chakra;
  > down your grounding cord (so the path looks like an inverted "U").

Take a few minutes to run Earth energy through the lower half of your body. Let the energy of Earth stimulate and release any blocked energies. Let yourself be aware of any different sensations you may experience.

After a minute or two, you can stop running Earth energy by just telling your energy to resume its normal flow.

Step II: Running Cosmic Energy

- Visualize your grounding cord. Bring your awareness into the present time and locate the center of your head. (Please refer to the section on "Grounding" if you need a quick review.)
- Ask your Crown (7th) chakra to open to a comfortable size and trust that it will do it.
- Imagine gold cosmic energy being pulled down through the top of your crown, entering your 7th chakra and traveling all the way down the back of your spine, through all the chakras until you reach the 1st chakra. Let the energy flow up the front of your spine and exit out the top of your head.

Take some time to run this Cosmic energy throughout your system, letting the gold energy flush out any blocked energies that can be released. You may notice as you run this kind of energy, that you feel lighter, that perhaps it's more challenging to keep your grounding cord in place, or that you may have a tendency to sway your body side to side. Just be aware of it, and when you're ready, stop running Cosmic energy by asking your energy to return to normal.

How did that feel? Do you feel more comfortable running one energy more than the other? Well, the truth is, you run both energies throughout your body at all times, except that in these exercises you ran them individually and in stronger proportions than normal. Usually you run your own individual mixture of Earth energy and Cosmic energy that your body has chosen. Your energy system decides what percentage of Earth energy to run and what percentage of Cosmic energy.

For meditation purposes you need to run more Cosmic energy than Earth energy to raise the vibrations. Why not run only Cosmic energy? You need to have Earth energy running to keep you connected to your body and to the planet, so healing can take place. The following is a "recipe" for running Cosmic and Earth energy as a form of meditation.

Step III: Running Cosmic and Earth Energy

- Visualize your grounding cord. Bring your awareness into the present time and locate the center of your head. (Please refer to the section on "Grounding" if you need a quick review.)
- Ask your feet, hand, and crown chakras to adjust to a size that is comfortable. Remember you don't have to think about it, the chakras know what size to adjust to.
- Start running Earth energy (see above for directions), only this time ask to draw in only 15 percent Earth energy. Keep running the 15 percent Earth energy throughout the lower portion of your body.
- Simultaneously as you run Earth energy, start bringing in Cosmic energy through the top of your crown (see above for directions). Ask to bring in 85 percent Cosmic energy so you're running 100 percent energy. (15 + 85 = 100).
- Both energies will meet in the 1st chakra. At that time, in the 1st chakra, the Earth and Cosmic mix together to create a combination energy.
- These combined energies will now circulate throughout your body in the following manner starting from the 1st chakra:

    Up the front of the spine, through the front of the chakras and out the top of your head where it "fountains" out into your aura;

    Up through your shoulders and arms traveling out each hand chakra;

    Down your hips and legs, traveling out your feet chakras;

    Any excess energy drains down your grounding cord to the center of Earth where the energy is sent back to its original source and Earth receives a healing.

While practicing this meditation you may become aware of slight pressure on the top of your head and/or shoulders. If you experience this, just lean forward and "dump energy." As a completion to the Running

Energy Meditation, I also recommend "dumping energy." This technique is explained below.

Step IV: Dumping Energy

- When you finish Running Energy, bend over at the waist and stretch your arms above your head.
- Gently lower your head and arms toward the ground, wiggle your fingers and toes, and let any excess energy from the top of your head and shoulders flow out into the earth where it will be transmuted into healing energy.
- Sit back up in your chair, open your eyes and bring yourself back to "normal."

When you first start practicing this meditation, do it only a few minutes at a time, gradually increasing your time until you are comfortable with twenty to thirty minutes a day. Once you are comfortable with the meditation, you can experiment with different ways of running energy as shown below.

Alternative Techniques

- Mix Earth and Cosmic energies in the 3rd chakra instead of the 1st chakra.
- Run Earth energy throughout entire body instead of just the lower portion as described above.
- Run Cosmic energy throughout entire body without any Earth energy.

The Running Energy Meditation is a very powerful technique and can bring about remarkable shifts in energy and attitude. In the following sections there are two more basic skills that can assist in releasing stuck energy and making the changes easier and more enjoyable.

Transforming Energy

The Running Energy Meditation is a super-powered clean out for your energy field and, as such, dislodges old issues and memories that at one time you chose to bury. These old memories and issues are sometimes referred to as "pictures" because they often appear as photographic images in your mind's eye. To avoid getting stuck in old pictures, or feeling overwhelmed by them, you need a way to dissolve them—to remove the emotional charge from them. This is one function the Transforming Energy Technique performs.

Pictures are charged with emotional energy until the charge is de-energized. The charge can be positive as well as negative. You have great memories as well as awful ones. When you see the mental image or picture and are reminded of the event, you energetically leave the present time and go to the past event. The moment you leave the present time, you lose your grounding, the ability to stay neutral, and are, at that moment, being controlled by that memory. Remember, creation and healing take place only in the present time, so it's important to have the ability to neutralize pictures to which you react, and come back to the here and now. You know you're reacting to a picture when you feel as if your buttons are being pushed. For example, you're talking with your friend, he or she says something, and you have a reaction that is far stronger than the situation warrants. Chances are that you are actually at the effect of an old picture that got "lit up" by your present situation. What you then want to do is to find the core picture and de-energize it. You'll know you've accomplished that when you find yourself in a similar situation and don't react, but remain neutral. There are hundreds, probably thousands, of pictures throughout your energy field so you'll never get bored running energy. Once one picture has been neutralized, the next one will light up. It's not a contest to see who can neutralize the most pictures in the least amount of time, so go at your own pace and be good to yourself.

Transforming Energy helps you maintain your equilibrium by neutralizing energy (negative or positive thought forms, feelings, emotions, patterns, programming—yours or someone else's) that may otherwise cause you to lose your grounding. Pictures light up throughout the day that can affect your grounding and your ability to function in an objective manner. You don't have to wait until you're running energy to perform this technique. This technique can and is encouraged to be done anytime, anywhere!

As mentioned above, your energy shifts as you practice the Running Energy Meditation, freeing previously stuck energy and circulating it throughout your energy field where it remains until it is released outside of your aura. Another function Transforming Energy performs is taking the energy that has remained in your aura and releasing and dispersing it outside your energy field, thereby transforming it into usable, healing energy and freeing you from unwanted influences of the past so you can create more of the reality you'd like for yourself in the present.

The following is a step-by-step guide for learning how to transform energy from a charged state to a neutral state. I mentioned earlier in the Protection section that you would learn to use the rose image in another way besides as a protective shield. You can use the image in this exercise to facilitate the transforming of energy.

A Transforming Energy Technique

1) Surround yourself with protection. Use the rose image if you'd like. (Please refer to the previous section on Protection if you'd like to review this technique.)

2) Ground. Bring yourself into present time and stay in the center of your head. (Please refer to the previous section on Grounding if you'd like to review this technique.)

3) Run Energy (Earth and Cosmic energy mix). (Please refer to the previous section, Running Energy Meditation, if you'd like to review this technique.)

4) Imagine a big, beautiful rose in front of you and outside your aura. The image of a rose is used because it is a universal symbol for love, transformation, and growth as represented by its blossoming from a bud

to full bloom, where it dies and regenerates. Remember your rose can be any color, size, or shape.

5) Place unwanted energy (emotion, situation, concept, person) into the center of the rose. You are not harming the person when you do this. You are merely taking the energy that person has left on you and giving it back to him or her.

6) Dissolve the rose. You can use whatever method you can think of to dissolve the rose into tiny particles of energy. Here are a couple of suggestions:

Visualize a stick of dynamite underneath the rose, light the fuse and let it explode. This method is very effective and has a certain appeal when you really want to get rid of that old energy. However, it is a rather aggressive approach, so if you're not comfortable with it, please find one that you're more comfortable with. There are more suggestions listed under Alternative Techniques.

You could also visualize a laser and "zap" the rose to dissolve it into tiny particles. Please remember you're not harming an actual rose or person, you are merely dissolving an image that represents programs, behavior, or emotions that you want to be freed from.

7) As tiny particles disperse, ask that anyone else's energy turn a color and send that energy back to its original source. The person gets his or her energy back and thus receives a healing.

8) Visualize a bright golden Sun above your head.

9) Place all the energy that belongs to you into that golden Sun. You can locate your scattered energy by simply calling for it, as you would a dog, and let it come to you. Because the energy may still contain remnants of other's energies, placing that energy into the burning, golden Sun purifies and neutralizes the energy making it ready for your use.

10) Take a deep breath, and on the exhale visualize the golden Sun expanding to fill your aura with this purified, revitalized energy.

11) Repeat Steps 3–10 for any situation for which you would like to gain neutrality. Remember you may have to dissolve an issue a number of

times before it is neutralized. It may take only once, or it could take hundreds of times, depending upon how deep the issue is and your willingness to let it go.

12) When finished, stop Running Energy and dump any excess energy into the earth for healing and transformation. (Please refer to Dumping Energy section of Running Energy Meditation.)

Alternative Techniques
Instead of, or in addition to, using roses for Transforming Energy you can:
- Visualize angels' hands lifting the energy.
- Visualize balloons lifting the energy all the way to the highest of highs or you can pop the balloon to transform the energy.
- Visualize placing the charged energy (issues, situations) in a suitcase and dissolve it.
- Visualize God's hands holding a ball of gold light and place the situation, person, or issue into the light.
- Visualize other types of flowers besides roses, and place the energy in the flower to be dissolved.
- Visualize a computer screen in front of you. Place the person, situation or issue into a folder on the screen and either dump the folder into the trash or press the command button to delete it.
- Burn sage, incense, or candles to help transform the energy in your surroundings and in your energy field.
- Place little bowls of salt water in the corners of the room to help absorb and transform any negativity in your surroundings.
- Sprinkle holy water on yourself and in the room to cleanse, purify, and transform the energy.
- Ring chimes. The sound vibration breaks up the negativity in the environment and your auric field.
- Laugh! A sense of humor helps! Don't take yourself too

seriously. Laughter shatters crystallized energy, helping you transform and heal.

Balancing Energy

When you practice the Running Energy Meditation and add the Transforming Energy Technique you are creating major changes in the way your energy system runs. You may go through a period of time where the majority of your focus is on issues related to one particular chakra, and that's normal. However, just like any situation where we focus on only one thing, an imbalance is created and something has to be done to restore balance. To use strength training as an example: if you focus only on developing your upper body, you'll soon notice that the upper body seems out of proportion to the lower body, because you haven't been working the hips, buttocks, or leg muscles. Thus an imbalance has been created. If this isn't addressed, your lower body eventually might not be able to support your body and it will find some other way to compensate for the imbalance. Your body is out of alignment and is not functioning to its full capacity. To remedy it, you balance your workouts to accommodate the needs of the lower body while still developing the chest, back, arms, and shoulders. The Balancing Energy Technique applies a similar principle, only to the energy system. It allows you to focus your healing on a specific chakra while balancing and stabilizing the rest of the chakras and brings them into alignment with each other as a fully functioning energy system. Balancing your energy restores the natural harmony of your body—a state of grace, stability, loving and balance. In this neutral state you can exercise your free will and function with greater clarity, awareness, and control.

This technique is wonderful to do on its own as a quick tune up, or as a final cleanout prior to completing the Running Energy Meditation, to bring all the chakras into balance.

An Energy Balancing Technique

You can visualize the following as you practice the Running Energy Meditation. Remember, when you visualize something, you are using your imagination to create an image in your mind's eye or to develop a sense of it to make it more real to you. (Please see the previous section on Running Energy Meditation should you need to review how to do the meditation.)

• Balancing the Chakras •

Start with your 1st chakra and move upward, completing steps 1–7 for each chakra. You begin this process with the 1st chakra because the lower three chakras have the most dense vibration, dealing primarily with the physical body and emotional issues, and usually require more attention than the upper chakras, which have a higher vibration that makes it easier to release blocks in the 5th, 6th, and 7th chakras.

1) Release any foreign energy that you're willing to let go of. Your willingness to let go of the energy is of key importance, because if you truly don't want to release it, it'll come right back. What I recommend you do to remove the foreign energy is a combination of visualization and actual physical movement. Place your hands a few inches away from the chakra, one in front of you and one behind you. (If you cannot physically reach behind you, that's okay, just use your imagination.) Feel around to sense where there may be stuck energy. With a sweeping motion of your hand, take that energy and flick it off into an imaginary rose that you've placed outside of your aura. Dissolve the rose. Repeat this a couple of times until you're ready to move on.

2) Clean out the chakra with cosmic gold energy by visualizing gold energy flowing through each chakra. You can even place your hands a minimum of 6 inches away from the chakra, one hand in front and the other behind you, and imagine gold energy flowing back and forth between your hands, flushing out the chakra.

3) Remove any "cords" of energy (see next section for more information about cords and how to remove them).

4) Bring the chakra into present time. Simply ask the chakra to come into present time and it will do it.

5) Fill up the chakra with your highest affinity. Place your hands a few inches away from the chakra, one hand in front and the other behind you. Visualize cosmic peach or pink, the colors of affinity, flowing between your hands, filling your chakra with affinity as a method of claiming the chakra for yourself or owning your space.

6) Fill up the chakra with cosmic gold energy. Keep your hands in the same position as above, and visualize (or imagine) gold energy flowing between your hands, filling the chakra with the gold vibration.

7) Ask the chakra to balance and stabilize itself and come into alignment with the rest of the chakras. You don't have to do anything, just setting the intention is enough.

8) Now you're ready to clean out the next chakra. So, start again with Step 1 and repeat Steps 1-7 until you've cleaned out all seven major chakras. Then you can clean out the secondary chakras in the arms and legs.

• Balancing the Arm and Leg Channels •

1) Visualize cosmic gold energy flowing from the back of your chest (behind the heart chakra) through your shoulders, arms, and out your elbow chakra;

2) Clean your elbow chakra by visualizing gold energy flowing through the chakra;

3) Ask your chakra to come into present time, balance and stabilize itself;

4) Visualize cosmic gold energy flowing from your elbow chakra to your hand chakra;

5) Clean your hand chakra by visualizing gold energy flowing through the chakra;

6) Ask your chakra to come into present time, balance and stabilize itself;

7) Repeat Steps 1–6 for the other arm, then move to the legs and do the following:

8) Visualize cosmic gold energy flowing from the back of your 2nd chakra into your knee chakra;

9) Clean your knee chakra by visualizing gold energy flowing through the chakra;

10) Ask your chakra to come into present time, balance and stabilize itself;

11) Visualize sending cosmic gold energy from your knee chakra to your foot chakra;

12) Clean your foot chakra by visualizing gold energy flowing through the chakra;

13) Ask your chakra to come into present time, balance and stabilize itself;

14) Repeat Steps 8–13 for the other leg.

Complete the Energy Balancing process by taking a deep breath, and on the exhale fill your aura with affinity (pink or peach color). Seal your aura by imagining gold energy surrounding and protecting you.

Alternative Techniques

For a quick cleanout, imagine a golden rose and use it as you would a bottle scrubber to clean out each chakra. Scrub in and out and side to side to get the chakra squeaky clean. Dissolve the rose as it gets dirty and replace it with a new, fresh gold rose before going on to the next chakra.

The remaining alternative energy balancing techniques are covered in more detail in the Chakra Therapies portion of this book:

- Crystals and gemstones
- Sound (singing, chanting, musical instruments)
- Exercise—yoga
- Color therapy
- Breathing exercises
- Aromatherapy

Cords

I have mentioned the concept of energy cords several times throughout this book and would now like to explain what they are and how to remove them. Simply put, cords are people's requests for attention. They are lines of energy, resembling a cord or string, that enter into one or more of your chakras and connect you with another person.

This is a very common practice between human beings, and on a more basic level, between animals and humans. Cording occurs all the time. Cords are passed back and forth between people's chakras constantly, without the people being aware of it. So, on a surface level, it's a good thing because it helps you to connect with others and not feel isolated. Carried to an extreme, however, it can be very destructive, leading to one person being controlled by another. If someone has a lot of cords, then he or she will operate partially on another's energy (influence) rather than on his or her own.

Please remember there are no victims here. A cord cannot be forced upon you. You cannot receive a cord from someone unless on some level you're willing to do so. It takes two to tango! So, the questions you ask yourself when you've been corded are: Do I want to keep this cord? If I don't want this cord, how did I participate in letting it in? What "picture" did it come in on?

You may want to leave some cords in for a while because they are relatively harmless and don't drain you of energy. An example of positive cording is the 2nd and 4th chakra ones passed between lovers. The 2nd chakra cord provides the sexual attraction and the 4th chakra cord involves the heart and relating in love. Also, the 1st chakra cord between mother and child is a positive cord and should remain because the baby is dependent on the mother for survival for the first year or two. Even your pets will cord you. I know my beloved cat has gotten me a number of times; walking down the aisle in the grocery store, I suddenly have to get cat food, even though he already has plenty at home. These are harmless examples of cording, and are ones that allow us to relate to each other.

There are other examples of more threatening cords, the ones that are manipulative and controlling. These are discussed earlier in the book and can be found in the Emotional, Mental and Physical Issues section and the Overview of the Chakra System section. These cords you do want to remove and here's a technique you can use to remove them.

Removing Cords

You can see, visualize, sense, or feel cords in the aura and chakras by slowly moving your hands along your chakras. As you scan your energy field, you may notice a difference in temperature, hot or cold; sense a thickening of the energy; feel a pulsing in your hand or heat in your hand, or you may just have a hunch that you have been corded. These are all indications of an energy block or of a cord blocking your energy. Listen to yourself; you will develop your own set of signals indicating where the imbalance is.

A cord can be big, small, thick, wispy, easy or difficult to remove. There are no set rules. However the best guideline is to be gentle when removing cords, as you don't want to tear a hole in your aura or chakra. Most cords will slide right out. Begin by locating the cord. Put your hand where you believe the cord is located. Imagine (visualize) the cord, and starting at your skin, gently twist the cord to one side and then pull it out with your hand (or you may visualize a hand doing this). Tie a knot at the end of the cord and throw it away (perhaps in a rose placed outside your aura), sending the energy back to its owner. Place your hand over the previously corded area and visualize filling it with cosmic gold energy to soothe and heal it.

If a cord seems stubborn, ask the cord who owns it, or mentally follow it out from the aura until you see, visualize, sense, or feel the person who sent it to you. When you've traced the cord back to its owner, thank him or her for the interest, and communicate that you do not want to be corded. If he or she wants to relate to you, tell him or her to do so on a conscious, physical plane instead of on the astral plane.

Chakra Therapies

The Running Energy Meditation covered in the last section is only one method of cleansing, energizing and balancing the chakras. This section focuses on seven other types of therapies that can be used in addition to, or instead of, the Running Energy Meditation to balance and open the chakras. All seven therapies will be represented under each chakra section. So, once you've identified which chakra is the most out of balance, you can turn to this Chakra Therapy section and look under that particular chakra to find the alternative therapies. Here's a brief explanation of the therapies offered.

Nature Therapy

Nature Therapy recommends different environmental settings that stimulate or relax the chakras. The optimal way of practicing Nature Therapy would be to meditate in the actual nature setting. However, since this may not always be feasible, the next best method is to imagine (or visualize) that you are in the suggested setting, or find a photograph that depicts the setting and gaze at it in contemplation. There are no rights or wrongs. Use your creativity to make the nature setting real for you.

Sound Therapy

This therapy includes music and vocal chants that create vibrations to which each chakra will respond. Music selection can be very subjective, and I encourage you to trust instinct and listen to music that makes you resonate. There are numerous tapes and compact discs available that contain music composed specifically to harmonize the chakras and produce feelings of serenity and peace. For example, the music of Ravi Shankar is designed to raise the energy vibrations of the chakras. There are also musical instruments to which you may feel drawn: drums, chimes, crystal bowls, or chakra tuning forks, to mention a few. Trust your instincts.

Your voice is an important instrument in sound therapy. Included in the sound therapy section of each chakra are vowel sounds that can be used to balance that particular chakra as well as the musical key to sing it in. Whether or not you believe you can sing doesn't matter. You have a voice that is beautiful and meant to be heard!

Color Therapy

Color Therapy embraces the concept that colors also contain certain vibrations that affect the energy of the chakras—opening, clearing, and balancing them. There are several ways you can approach this therapy.

The first is by visualizing the recommended color and breathing it into your body. Focus on the chakra and then breathe the color into that chakra, letting the color fill your body and aura. You can also visualize the color and place it in a ball above your crown chakra (the top of your head), while practicing the Running Energy Meditation. This is a wonderful clearing technique. If the color recommended in this book doesn't feel right to you, that's okay. Just ask your body what color it does want, trust the answer you get, and breathe that color into your energy field. When you "see" a color, you are actually perceiving a vibration. That vibration may mean "blue" to me but you may "see" it as green. We are both experiencing the same vibration, but we associate it with different words.

Another way to experience color therapy is to wear clothing the color of the chakra you want to relax or activate. If you can wear it where the chakra is located that's even better. Another variation is to surround yourself in your environment with colors that complement your energy and give you the results you want.

Aromatherapy

Aromatherapy, the study of scent, is the skilled and controlled use of essential oils for physical and emotional health and well-being. Essential oils are either applied to the skin or inhaled. Your sense of smell is one of the most powerful senses and can have a profound effect on your healing and ability to release and relax. Certain fragrances can stimulate or relax specific chakras, and can facilitate healing emotional and physical issues affiliated with each chakra.

Aromatherapy is quite an exciting and extensive field of study. I encourage you to research it further if it interests you. In the Recommended Reading List at the back of the book, I have suggested several books for your reference.

Here are a few ways to use essential oils: You can add a couple of drops of essential oil to water and heat the water in order to inhale the vapors; add drops of oil to your bath and soak in it; add drops of oil to massage oil or lotion and massage it into your skin; or you can invest in an aromatic diffuser designed to be used with these oils. Discover the methods that work best for you and enjoy!

Reflexology

This is the stimulation of reflex zones through pressure point massage. We have many reflex systems throughout the body (hands, ears, face, and eyes) that correspond with different organs in the body. The most common and widely used zone is the foot. The reflex zones in your feet happen to correspond with the seven major chakras. To practice this therapy simply massage the recommended zone and pressure points with your fingers, using a gentle, circular motion.

Gemstone and Crystal Therapy

This therapy uses the vibrational healing influence of particular gemstones and crystals to activate or relax specific chakras. Each crystal and gemstone emits a vibration that resonates with the energies of different chakras and their related health issues. This therapy is easy to do: simply place the gemstone or crystal of your choice (that corresponds with the chakra you want to balance) on your body where the chakra is located. Keep it there for as long as you need. You can also carry the particular crystal or gemstone with you, or wear it around your neck. Another variation is to lie down in a comfortable position (face up) and place one gemstone or crystal on each of the corresponding chakras and balance all seven chakras at once. Lie in this position for about 20 minutes. The effects vary depending upon how sensitive you are to crystals and gemstones. Remember, most gemstones and crystals resonate to more than one chakra. The gemstones and crystals you use for balancing will change according to what's happening in your life at the time.

When using crystals for healing, it's a good idea to cleanse them first. There are a number of ways to accomplish this. One of the best ways is to place them in salt water overnight. If water from the ocean is not available, you can make your own salt water by mixing sea salt and water together in a bowl. A quick cleaning can be done by holding the gemstones and crystals under running water, or lighting sage and waving the crystal or gemstone through the smoke of the burning sage.

Remember, as always, to follow your own inner guidance and innate ability to heal.

Common Fitness Exercises

As a fitness and aerobics instructor, I can attest to the healthy benefits of regular exercise. What I have discovered through the years is that many of the "common" exercises and stretches that I teach everyday in fitness classes can be slightly modified to consciously balance and energize the chakra system. Most of the stretches have their roots in yoga, so they need little modification.

Included in this section is an "everyday" exercise that I have found to have positive influence on the chakras. Not only do the exercises assist with balancing the chakras, they also strengthen and tone the body!

Yoga Therapy

A book on chakra therapy would not be complete without including something about the practice of yoga. Albeit I will only scratch the surface of this vast field, it is definitely worthy of note. The term "yoga" comes from the Sanskrit word *yuj* meaning "to join, integrate or make whole."

The most popular form of yoga in the Western world is Hatha Yoga or "the yoga of health." This yoga focuses primarily on breathing and postures. The yoga postures (*asanas*) that I mention under Yoga Therapy come from the Hatha Yoga tradition and can be learned and researched further by attending yoga classes, watching one of the many yoga videos available, or studying yoga through books. Choose the best method of learning based upon your individual needs and learning skills. In my opinion, attending classes is a superior method of learning since the teacher is there to personally assist you and ensure that you are practicing the postures using proper form and technique.

Yoga exercises restore harmony and tranquillity to the mind, body, and spirit. The yoga breathing exercises encourage and train you to shift your attention away from distracting stimuli and to focus instead on the breathing process. This has a calming effect on your entire system and helps you regain a sense of self-control.

There a several types of yoga, yet they are so closely interlinked it is nearly impossible to practice only one pure form of yoga. Six of the seven chakras have a yoga practice associated with them. For each chakra I will briefly share the nature of its affiliated yoga practices. Certain yoga postures are known to have beneficial effect on emotional and physical disorders related to the chakras. I will list a few of the postures for each chakra under Yoga Therapy, however, due to the parameters of this book, I will not describe how to do all the poses. For more information on yoga practice please refer to the Recommended Reading List at the back of this book.

When performing any of the yoga postures recommended, I suggest wearing comfortable clothing, using a mat or folded blanket on the floor underneath you for comfort and safety, breathing deeply into the abdomen through the nose not the mouth, and maintaining an attitude of "mindfulness."

Chakra Therapies for the
1ST CHAKRA

Nature Therapy

Sit on the ground with your legs crossed in the lotus position. This position brings the 1st chakra (located at the base of your spine) in direct contact with Earth and thus provides a grounding effect. Look at or imagine the beautiful red and orange colors that appear in the sky at sunset and at sunrise. Let the beauty and harmony of this natural display of color bring rejuvenation into your 1st chakra. Feel it spread warmth throughout the entire chakra system and body. The beautiful red and orange colors gently stimulate your senses, awaken the fire, the passion inside of you for life.

Sound Therapy

Listening to music that contains a steady, driving, and forceful rhythm awakens the primal energy forces of the 1st chakra. Drumming raises this energy throughout, at times leading to a ritualistic, ecstatic dance as the energy surges. You can even witness this on the dance floor in music clubs when the music has a driving bass or drumbeat. To relax the 1st chakra, listen to the sounds of nature—birds singing, crickets chirping, frogs croaking in a rhythm attuned to nature.

Vocally you can chant the vowel "u" spoken as "ooh," or you can sing it in the key of lower C.

Color Therapy

Clear bright red is used for this chakra. The red color warms, revitalizes, and awakens the life force energy. I suggest the lighter, brighter end of the red color spectrum rather than bluish reds, as the darker reds are oftentimes associated with depression and unexpressed anger. As always, check it out for yourself.

Aromatherapy

A few of the scents that can be used to activate the 1st chakra, reduce depression, stimulate circulation, and generate warmth are rose, jasmine, patchouli, and sandalwood. To improve your connection with Earth, you could try cedar. Clove is wonderful for dissolving blocked energies.

Reflexology

Locate the pressure point on your heel and slightly to the inside. Gently massage. Apply steady pressure to the spot to stimulate the chakra and release energy blocks.

Gemstones and Crystals

Agate, Bloodstone, Black Tourmaline, Garnet, Hematite, Obsidian, Pyrite, Red Coral, Red Jasper, Ruby, Smoky Quartz, Snowflake Obsidian.

• *Transformational Qualities of Gemstones and Crystals* •

AGATE: Makes it easier to recognize truth and find acceptance; grounding and energizing stone; blends and unites energies for strength and protection; potent healer.

BLACK TOURMALINE: Drives away fear and negativity; provides protection; supports concentration and increases sensitivity and understanding; powerful healer; helps anchor higher vibrations into the physical body; helps develop inner wisdom, self-mastery, serenity, and strength; activates adrenal glands and positively affects the spinal column, colon, and legs.

BLOODSTONE: Contains protective qualities that prevent injury and illness; increases physical stamina and mental alertness; diminishes emotional and mental stress; powerful healer for the physical body with ailments such as headaches, high blood pressure, cardiac arrest, and kidneys; influences inner guidance and the desire to be of service.

GARNET: Strengthens, purifies, and energizes the body; aids circulation, increases sex drive, and balances thyroid disorders; enhances capacity for love and compassion, use of imagination, and reduces feelings of insecurity; dispels negativity increases initiative and will power.

HEMATITE: Provides strength and vitality; increases resistance to stress; strengthens charisma, optimism, self-control, and courage; dissolves negative energy and works as a protective shield from outside forces; helps circulate oxygen throughout body; decreases inflammation, draws out heat from a feverish part of the body.

OBSIDIAN (BLACK): Helps integrate the mind with the emotions and anchors spiritual energy onto the physical plane; absorbs and dissolves negative energy; prevents emotional draining from others; reduces stress; helps clear underlying blocks and helps soothe during times of transition; helps us to touch and embrace those deep places within ourselves that are not usually acknowledged, accepted, or nurtured; beneficially influences stomach, colon, womb.

PYRITE: Used to aid digestion and improve oxygen flow to the body; influences a more positive outlook on life; enhances emotional wellbeing and self-control; helps your ability to work harmoniously with others, as it assists in matching your vibrations with someone else.

RED CORAL: Brings flow, stability, and balance to the emotions; assists you in being more positive in your attitude, emotional outlook, and creative expression; increases your sensitivity to and awareness of the Self, others, and life in general.

RED JASPER: Powerful healer for the physical body; strengthens blood, enhances vitality, and sense of security, strength and patience; reduces anxiety; increases your sensitivity to Earth and helps you ground to it; represents Earth energy.

RUBY: Intensifies feelings of love and compassion; stimulates sex drive; emphasizes courage, forthrightness, service orientation, spiritual focus, power, and leadership; aids regeneration of the physical heart, and energizes blood and entire energy system.

SMOKY QUARTZ: Balances sexual energy; aids in relieving the effects of depression; dissolves blocks and negativity on all levels; enhances ability to remember your dreams and opens you to your channeling abilities; helps you ground to Earth and center yourself.

SNOWFLAKE OBSIDIAN: Similar qualities as black obsidian, but less intense; encourages you to adopt a lighter approach to exploring your inner depths; the black and white color represents the balance and true oneness of polarities (male/female, spirit/matter, dark/light, positive/negative).

Yoga Therapy

There are two yogas associated with the 1st chakra—Hatha Yoga and Kundalini Yoga. As mentioned before, Hatha Yoga is the most common yoga practiced in Western society. Traditionally, Hatha Yoga is regarded as preparation for other yogas. It purifies the consciousness indirectly through the body using breath, posture, and muscle control. Hatha Yoga techniques cleanse the bloodstream, tissues, glands, and nervous system, creating harmony and balance.

The word "hatha" is derived from *ha,* meaning "sun," and *tha,* meaning "moon." Breath inhaled through the right nostril is referred to as "sun breath" and breath through the left nostril is "moon breath." Through the focus of breath, you balance the positive (sun) and negative (moon)—the male/female, yin/yang polarities.

Kundalini (Serpent Power) Yoga is the other yoga affiliated with the 1st chakra. According to Yogic tradition, "kundalini" is the life-force energy that lies dormant at the base of the spine. It is represented symbolically as a serpent. Through predominantly breathing exercises and posture (muscle) the idea is to awaken the kundalini energy within and raise it by channeling the energy chakra by chakra to the highest chakra where bliss consciousness (samadhi) is achieved. This is a very complex process that takes years, if not a lifetime, to achieve. Because of its complex nature and inherent danger, a qualified teacher's supervision is strongly recommended.

• *Recommended Yoga Postures* •

BACKACHE: Back Stretching, Bow, Cobra, Cow Face, Spinal Twist
SCIATICA: Big Toe
CANCER: Sun Salutation

Physical and Breathing Exercises

• *Common Physical Exercise: Half Squat* •

Visualize a column of energy from the base of your spine going all the way to the middle of the earth where it anchors. This is your grounding. Now do the following exercise:

1) You can use a chair if you'd like. Stand about 1 foot in front of the chair, facing away from it. Place your feet shoulder-width apart, toes pointed slightly out. Make sure your knees are in alignment with (directly over) your ankles to avoid stressing your knee joints. Shift the weight of your body over your heels (not your toes).

2) Start lowering your hips by bending your knees, as if you're going to sit down in the chair. Your buttocks will be sticking out behind you. Lower your hips and buttocks until they barely touch the seat of the chair.

3) Contract your abdominal muscles, squeeze your buttocks together, and lift yourself back up to a standing position.

4) Repeat 8 times. Rest and do another set of 8.

Variation: Perform the same exercise but place your toes facing forward instead of angled slightly outward.

• *Yoga Posture: Star Posture* •

1) Sit comfortably erect with legs extended in front of you, and breathe regularly (see figure 5, page 111).

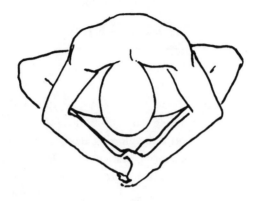

Figure 5. Star Posture.

2) Bend your right knee in toward your chest, and place the sole of your foot opposite your left knee. Maintain this distance between foot and body when doing the rest of the exercise.

3) Bend your left knee and bring the soles of your feet together, allowing your knees to fall gently toward the floor.

4) Clasp your hands around your feet without shifting their position.

5) Exhale, slowly bending forward. Lower your face toward your feet until you reach a point of mild tension. Hold in that position and breathe into the stretch.

6) Hold the position for as long as you comfortably can. Breathe regularly.

7) Slowly resume your starting position, breathing gently into each movement.

8) Rest.

Chakra Therapies for the
2ND CHAKRA

Nature Therapy
Relax in a body of water, feeling the water soothe you and lift you as it flows around your body, washing away any tensions or negativity. As you look into the night sky, notice the glowing moonlight as it reflects off the water. Let the moon's nurturing beam of light help balance the feminine energies of the second chakra. Oftentimes emotions are symbolically represented by water, so it is only appropriate that water would be one of the forms of relaxing and healing the emotional center, the 2nd chakra.

Sound Therapy
Similar to the concept of flowing water, to relax the 2nd chakra you want to listen to music that seems to flow, is harmonious and soothing. There are a number of tapes and compact discs available that combine this soothing type of music with the sounds of ocean surf, waterfalls, rainfall, and running water to produce a very powerful sound therapy tool for this chakra.

Vocally you can chant the vowel "o" spoken as in "November," or you can sing it in the key of D.

Color Therapy
For the 2nd chakra, clear orange is used to stimulate and renew your energy. It facilitates your letting go of rigid emotional patterns, and lifts your self-esteem.

Aromatherapy
A few scents that can be used to balance the emotions, improve digestion (the ability to "let go" and release) and ease stress are bergamot, vanilla, bitter almond, and sandalwood. Ylang-ylang stimulates sensuality and is often used to help "set the mood" for a romantic encounter with your loved one.

Reflexology

Locate the pressure point immediately above the inside heel, but not yet at the arch of the foot. Massage, applying gentle, steady pressure to the point to release blocked energies in the 2nd chakra.

Gemstones and Crystals

Amber, Carnelian, Citrine, Coral, Moonstone, Gold Calcite, Gold Topaz, Peach Aventurine.

• *Transformational Qualities of Gemstones and Crystals* •

AMBER: Has a positive influence on the hormones, spleen and heart; promotes healing and purification of the digestive tract; absorbs negative energy, helps you to ground to Earth, and provides protection for sensitive people; blends and balances the higher intellect with spirituality.

CARNELIAN: Energizes the blood in your body, stimulates life force energy, physical power, and fortitude; helps you ground to the physical, enhances communication with your Higher Self, and helps concentration; opens your heart with warmth and joy.

CITRINE: Excellent stone for healing ailments of the kidneys, heart, digestive organs, colon, and liver; helps body eliminate toxins; reduces self-destructive behavior, instills a feeling of stability; elevates self-esteem and enhances alignment with Higher Self; attracts abundance, helps you ground to the present time.

CORAL: Provides steadiness, flow, and balance to your emotional well-being; helps you maintain a more positive outlook on life, gain a new perspective, and express creatively; increases your sensitivity to those around you.

GOLD CALCITE: Balances your emotions and the male/female polarities within you; reduces stress, alleviates fear and anxiety, and grounds excess energy so you feel more calm; great to wear when you need to be mentally focused and alert.

GOLD TOPAZ: Strengthens the functions of the liver, nervous system, and digestive organs; helps relieve tension headaches, muscle spasms and mental nervousness; provides relief and balance for those who've suffered from a mental or emotional breakdown, or from anyone experiencing extreme stress, nervous or mental fatigue; assists with the process of letting go and accepting change.

MOONSTONE: Heals physical disorders related to the stomach, pancreas and lymphatic system; relieves anxiety and stress, helps calm you in times of emotional stress or when you overreact emotionally; promotes a flexible attitude and aligns your emotions with your Higher Self.

PEACH AVENTURINE: Helps you let go of anxiety, worry, and uncertainty; evokes emotional calm and a positive attitude toward life; helps you find your center and align with it; enhances your intuition, insights, sense of individuality, good health, and positive well-being.

Yoga Therapy

Tantrism, the Yoga of Sex is very aptly associated with the 2nd chakra. Tantrism takes its name from the Tantras, scriptures which were written to provide instruction for ritual and contemplation. Tantrism requires long preparatory training and careful initiation into its practices. Because of its sexual content, many people in the past have misinterpreted the practices and abused the privileges. Thus, authentic Tantric practice and ritual has become a closely guarded secret.

Tantrism as a yoga practice aims at harnessing the powerful forces of sexual energy for the purpose of achieving higher consciousness. There are two schools of thought on this. The first school achieves the state of higher consciousness by concentrating and conserving the sexual energy through celibacy; choosing instead to channel the sexual energy for meditation and spiritual purposes. For this practice, even the seminal fluid is sacred and not to be wasted.

The second school views sexual union itself as a sacred means of achieving higher awareness. The physical union between a man and woman in love and mindfulness is a spiritual path itself. Coitus, in this school, becomes a sacrament. Another unique quality of Tantric philosophy is its willingness to enthusiastically embrace life and experience the dance of life in its entirety.

• *Recommended Yoga Postures* •

REPRODUCTIVE ORGANS: Back Stretching, Cobra, Plough, The Butterfly
PROSTATE: Spinal Twist, The Butterfly, Shoulder Stand
ADDICTION: Sun Salutation, Balance Posture, Pose of Tranquillity

Physical and Breathing Exercises

• *Common Physical Exercise: Abdominal Curl with a Twist* •

1) Lie on your back, legs hip-width apart, with your knees bent and pointing toward the ceiling. Let the floor support you. Feel your lower back against the floor.

2) Bring your hands behind your head, gently cradling your neck and head with your hands. Relax your neck. To relieve tension in the neck, you might try placing the tip of your tongue on the roof of your mouth right behind your front teeth. This assists you in breathing properly so you can focus your attention on your abdominal muscles rather than letting the neck do the work, and thus straining your neck.

3) Contract your abdominal muscles by pressing your lower back into the floor and lift the bent right knee in toward your chest. Simultaneously, lift your left shoulder off the floor, lead with your shoulder, not your elbow, and bring your shoulder toward the right knee (opposite shoulder to opposite knee). This is the inhale motion.

4) Now exhale as you straighten your right leg, pressing out through the heel, while lowering your shoulder back to the floor.

5) Repeat this move 8–10 times.

6) Change sides, bringing your left knee in toward your right shoulder. Repeat this move 8–10 times.

Variation: Alternate your legs as if you are riding a bicycle. Remember to keep breathing and maintain lower back contact with the floor to sup-

port your back and isolate the abdominal muscles. Remember to inhale
on the way up and exhale on the way down.

• *Yoga Posture: The Camel* •

1) Come into a kneeling position with your legs together, toes pointing
backward.

2) Bring your hands to your waist, supporting your lower back, and very
carefully tilt your head backward.

3) Slowly and with careful awareness, place your right hand on your right
heel behind you, and then place your left hand on your left heel (see figure 6). Keep your hips elevated (don't let them sag).

4) Breathe regularly and hold this position for as long as is comfortable
for you.

5) Release by slowly and carefully resuming your starting position
(kneeling).

6) Rest (you might want to bend forward to stretch your back afterward).

Figure 6. The Camel Posture.

Chakra Therapies for the
3RD CHAKRA

Nature Therapy

Spend some time in the radiant golden sunlight of the outdoors to warm and stimulate the 3rd chakra. The sun is considered to contain "masculine" energies, promoting action and confidence. To manifest the abundance that is truly yours, you can contemplate a ripe field of wheat, bathing in the sunlight, gently blowing in the wind, representing "golden" opportunities that are yours daily.

Sound Therapy

To stimulate the 3rd chakra, to "get you going," listen to fiery orchestral music such as Antonio Vivaldi's "The Four Seasons" Concerto in F Minor, Op. 8, No. 4 (Winter). Orchestral music (particularly the string section) that is mellow, with an even tempo, will relax and calm the 3rd chakra.

Vocally you can chant the vowel open "o" spoken as in the word "God," or you can sing it in the key of E.

Color Therapy

Clear sunny yellow is used for the 3rd chakra to warm, invigorate, and create joy and cheerful relaxation. Yellow is considered to be a happy color (consider the popular smiley face), and lifts the mood, creating an optimistic outlook on life. When a golden hue is added to this yellow color, it becomes a potent healing vibration, clarifying and releasing psychological disorders.

Aromatherapy

A few of the scents that can be used to enhance the ability to let go, stimulate the intellect, and treat mental and physical exhaustion are lemon, acacia, lavender, rosemary, and bergamot. These will assist in stimulating and balancing the energies in the 3rd chakra.

Reflexology

Locate the pressure point right in the middle of the sole of your foot—the arch. Hold steady, gentle pressure as you massage the point to invigorate and relax blocks in the 3rd chakra and those organs associated with it.

Gemstones and Crystals

Amber, Aquamarine, Carnelian, Citrine, Emerald, Gold, Gold Calcite, Malachite, Peridot, Pyrite, Smoky Quartz, Tiger's-eye, Topaz.

• *Transformational Qualities of Gemstones and Crystals* •

AMBER: Has a positive influence on the hormones, spleen, and heart; promotes healing and purification of the digestive tract; absorbs negative energy, helps you to ground to Earth and provides protection for sensitive people; blends and balances the higher intellect with spirituality.

AQUAMARINE: Calms nervous tension, reduces retention of body fluids, and helps with digestion; increases clarity and facilitates creative self-expression; helps drive away fears and anxiety; soothes, calms, and tranquilizes; wonderful stone to use with meditation; creates balance on all levels: physical, emotional, and mental.

CARNELIAN: Energizes the blood in your body, stimulates life force energy, physical power and fortitude; helps you ground to the physical, enhances communication with your Higher Self and helps your concentration; opens your heart with warmth and joy.

CITRINE: Excellent stone for healing ailments of the kidneys, heart, digestive organs, colon, and liver; helps your body eliminate toxins; reduces self-destructive behavior and instills a feeling of stability; elevates self-esteem and enhances alignment with your Higher Self; attracts abundance and helps you ground to the present time.

EMERALD: Strengthens the immune system, heart, liver, kidneys, and nervous system; increases your ability to remember information received in dreams and during meditation, which provides you with deeper spiritual and personal insight; heightens memory, clairvoyance, wisdom, and increases intellect; represents your spiritual potential; enhances creative expression, love, balance, and patience.

GOLD: Purifies and rejuvenates the physical body; improves circulatory and nervous systems; balances and opens heart chakra; stimulates tissue regeneration; magnetizes positive energy to you; increases inner awareness.

GOLD CALCITE: Balances your emotions and the male/female polarities within you; reduces stress, alleviates fear and anxiety, and grounds excess energy so you feel calmer; great to wear when you need to be mentally focused and alert.

GOLD TOPAZ: Strengthens the functions of the liver, nervous system, and digestive organs; helps relieve tension headaches, muscle spasms, and mental nervousness; provides relief and balance for those who've suffered from a mental or emotional breakdown, or for anyone experiencing extreme stress and nervous or mental fatigue; assists you with the process of letting go and accepting change.

MALACHITE: Strengthens heart and circulatory system; aids weight loss; decreases stress and tension; stimulates tissue regeneration. energizes body and mind; brings unconscious blocks to light; balances on all levels: physical, mental, emotional.

PERIDOT: Has healthy impact upon heart, adrenals, pancreas, and liver; purifies your body; heightens intuition; decreases tension; helps calm you if you have a tendency toward stage fright or performance anxiety; speeds up your personal growth, stimulates mental capabilities, and opens heart and mind to new opportunities; soothes and releases old hurts and resentments.

PYRITE: Used to aid digestion and improve the oxygen flow to the body; influences a more positive outlook on life; enhances your emotional well-being and self-control; helps your ability to work harmoniously with others as it assists you in matching your vibrations with someone else.

SMOKY QUARTZ: Balances sexual energy; aids in relieving the effects of depression; dissolves blocks and negativity on all levels; enhances your ability to remember your dreams and opens you to your channeling abilities; helps you ground to Earth and center yourself.

TIGER'S EYE: Helpful for ailments involving the digestive organs, colon, spleen, or pancreas; heightens awareness of your higher potential and free choice; enhances ability to gain clear and objective insights; aids self-confidence and ability to be neutral; helps you ground to Earth and center yourself within yourself.

Yoga Therapy

Karma Yoga, the "Yoga of Action," is associated with your power center, the 3rd chakra. "Karma" means action, a special kind of mindful action that stems from non-attachment, a selfless service without thoughts of personal gain or recognition. Through practicing Karma Yoga you open yourself up to your higher purpose and bring your actions into alignment with it.

The attitude of one who practices this yoga is that of wisdom and love. Whether you are scrubbing toilets or performing brain surgery, both actions are equal when performed with the right attitude of compassion, love, and devotion to being of service to God and humanity in the here and now. You demonstrate this yoga philosophy when you are able to perform the task in front of you with devotion and without expectation of reward.

• *Recommended Yoga Postures* •

STOMACH: Mountain Posture, Pose of Tranquillity, The Tree
INDIGESTION: Cobra, Spinal Twist, Pose of Tranquillity
ANOREXIA: Pose of Tranquillity, Back Stretching, Cobra, Spinal Twist

Physical and Breathing Exercises

• *Common Physical Exercise: Upper Abdominal Curl* •

1) Lie on your back, legs hip-width apart with your knees bent and pointing toward the ceiling. Lift your legs off of the floor, so that your knees are bent at a 90 degree angle and cross your ankles. Let the floor

support you. Feel your lower back against the floor. This is the start position.

2) Fold your arms across your chest. Tuck your chin into your chest as if you're holding an orange in place.

3) Exhale, and to a count of two, slowly lift your shoulder blades off the floor, pressing your lower back into the floor as you lift up. Your shoulders will only be 1 to 1-1/2 inches off the floor. As you lift up, visualize your navel pressing down into your spine and into the floor to isolate the abdominal muscles.

4) Hold for a count of two, and then exhale slowly to a count of two, lowering your shoulder blades back to the floor.

5) Repeat: up for two, hold for two, and lower for two. Remember to exhale on the way up, and inhale on the way down.

6) Repeat 8 times.

Variations: Changing the position of your arms will affect the difficulty of this exercise. You can place your hands on your thighs and let them slide up your thighs as you lift your upper body off the floor. You can also place your hands behind your head, gently cradling your neck and head with your hands as you lift up.

• *Yoga Posture: Spinal Twist* •

1) Sit up nice and tall, spine comfortably erect, with your legs extended in front of you. Breathe regularly.

2) Bend your right leg at the knee and place your right foot to the outside of your left knee (see figure 7 on page 122). Keep breathing.

3) On an exhale, slowly and smoothly turn your upper body to the right, placing both hands on the floor at your right side. Turn your head and look over your right shoulder.

Figure 7. The spinal twist.

4) Continue breathing regularly and hold this position for as long as you comfortably can.

5) Release and slowly come back to center, returning to your starting position.

6) Repeat Steps 2–5 in the opposite direction.

Chakra Therapies for the
4TH CHAKRA

Nature Therapy

Take a stroll in the countryside, the rolling hills are lush and green from the fresh rainfall. Breathe in that richness of green growth and feel the healing energy as it encourages your heart to open up. Now walk a little further and notice the beautiful pink-colored flowers blooming on the hillsides. Experience the hopefulness, the optimism of the pink flowers. As you look up, perhaps you notice the sky is a pink color filled with gossamer clouds. Let the wonders of nature bring healing, hope, and affinity into your heart chakra.

Sound Therapy

Music that touches your heart is what will relax and open the 4th chakra. Whether it's classical, new age, or sacred music from the Eastern or Western traditions, let the music generate a warmth inside your heart. This is very subjective, so I encourage you to go with your heart and trust your own instinct on this.

Vocally you can chant "ah," or you can sing it in the key of F.

Color Therapy

Green is used for the 4th chakra to promote regeneration, new growth, inner peace, and serenity. Pink is also used, since its gentle, tender vibrations can loosen tension in the heart, and awaken feelings of love and tenderness as well as the childlike feelings of wonder, innocence, and happiness.

Aromatherapy

As the heart opens, true healing begins. With that in mind, scents used to facilitate greater healing, instill harmony and balance, cleanse and soothe the entire system, and increase vitality are mint, sage, musk, tuberose, ginger and rose.

Reflexology

Locate the pressure point right on the ball of your foot. Gently press and massage with a circular motion to release the energy blocks.

Gemstones and Crystals

Carnelian, Chrysophase, Emerald, Green Aventurine, Jade, Kunzite, Malachite, Rhodochrosite, Rhodonite, Rose Quartz, Ruby, Tourmaline.

• *Transformational Qualities of Gemstones and Crystals* •

CARNELIAN: Energizes the blood in your body, stimulates life force energy, physical power, and fortitude; helps you ground to the physical, enhances communication with your Higher Self, and helps your concentration; opens your heart with warmth and joy.

CHRYSOPHASE: Calms irrational, compulsive behavior patterns, relieves the effects of depression, and balances sexual disorders; promotes harmony, passion, and unconditional love; provides healing for all levels: physical, emotional, and mental; helps you gain clarity and insight into personal problems; brings inner gifts and talents to light.

EMERALD: Strengthens your immune system, heart, liver, kidneys, and nervous system; increases your ability to remember information received in dreams and during meditation, which provides you with deeper spiritual and personal insight; heightens memory, clairvoyance, wisdom, and increases intellect; represents your spiritual potential; enhances creative expression, love, balance, and patience.

GREEN AVENTURINE: Helps you let go of anxiety, worry, and uncertainty; evokes emotional calm and a positive attitude toward life; helps you find your center and align with it; enhances intuition, insights, sense of individuality, good health, and positive well-being.

JADE: Helps purify your blood system and relieves digestive disorders; increases life span, productivity, and creativity; promotes discernment, humility, courage, fair-mindedness, and wisdom; drives away negativity and encourages peace, serenity, and nurturance; if you are feeling nervous or are suffering from insomnia, jade can help you get a peaceful night's sleep and have pleasant dreams.

KUNZITE: Kunzite is helpful to people with addictions, suffering from manic depression, or displaying addictive behavior, as it contains a high level of lithium, which naturally soothes, calms, and balances; encourages receptivity, opening your heart chakra to God's love (Divine love), and surrendering to a Higher Power.

MALACHITE: Strengthens heart and circulatory system; aids weight loss; decreases stress and tension; stimulates tissue regeneration; energizes body and mind; brings unconscious blocks to light; balances on all levels: physical, mental, emotional.

RHODOCHROSITE: Heightens awareness and mental acuity; restores balance during times of emotional and physical crisis; helps heal emotional wounds and bridge the aspects of the lower chakras with the loving expression of the heart; enhances self-love and love and compassion for others.

RHODONITE: Has a calming influence during times of pain; restores physical energy and increases sense of self-worth; brings root chakra into alignment with the heart chakra in order to manifest Divine love on this physical planet; the variety of Rhodonite that is only pink deepens the comprehension that vulnerability is not a sign of weakness but actually an indicator of great strength.

ROSE QUARTZ: Encourages gentleness, tenderness, and love; teaches you to accept and love yourself and opens your heart for all expressions of love and tenderness within; it is regarded as the "Love Stone," dealing with all matters of the heart: love, affection, compassion, and kindness. It eases sexual and emotional imbalances; helps release stored anger, resentment, guilt, fear, and jealousy; aids your ability to forgive and accept with compassion and love; reduces stress and tension; cools hot tempers.

RUBY: Intensifies feelings of love and compassion; stimulates sex drive; emphasizes courage, forthrightness, service orientation, spiritual focus, power, and leadership; aids regeneration of the physical heart, and energizes blood and entire energy system.

TOURMALINE (GREEN): Produces a healthy, balanced expression of love and compassion; assists you in letting go of emotional pain and uncertainty; draws out toxins from the body and attracts new, rejuvenating energy; has soothing, balancing, and renewing influences during times of emotional transition, exhaustion, or stress; promotes acceptance, serenity, abundance, and prosperity.

TOURMALINE (PINK-GREEN): Balances opposite extremes, restoring harmony to the conflicting energies, as in the male/female polarities inside of you and reflected in your relationships; assists you in letting go of old emotional wounds so you can attract new, healthy love.

TOURMALINE (RED-PINK): Enhances ability to effectively handle life's challenges and meet new ones with courage, optimism, grace, and ease; helps you let go of grief, guilt, and anxiety; inspires acts of compassion, devotion, service, and creativity.

Yoga Therapy

The yoga associated with the 4th chakra is Bhakti Yoga, or the "Yoga of Devotion." Its purpose is to help you dissolve your ego and find your true Self. This practice has a more meditative form with its use of mantras. Bhakti yoga purifies the consciousness: the ever-present flame of Bhakti love burns up qualities considered to be spiritually undesirable and impure, such as hatred, anger, greed, pride, and other destructive emotions.

Bhakti Yoga is a favored yoga in India, requiring a simplicity of heart, willingness, and an unshakable devotion. Its practice opens you up to your heart's will, guidance, and wisdom.

• *Recommended Yoga Postures* •

ASTHMA: Mountain Posture, Pose of Tranquillity, Lotus, Bow
BRONCHITIS: Cobra, Mountain Posture, Fish, Shoulder Stand
HEART DISEASE: Pose of Tranquillity, Mountain Pose, Cleansing Breath
BLOOD PRESSURE: Pose of Tranquillity, Cleansing Breath

Physical and Breathing Exercises

• *Common Physical Exercise: Shoulder Rolls/Back Stroke* •

1) Stand up straight, feet shoulder-width apart, knees slightly bent, abdominal muscles pulled in, and hips tucked slightly under.

2) Lead with your right shoulder. Inhale as you lift the right shoulder up toward the ears and continue circling it toward the back, lowering the shoulder and leading it forward to complete one full rotation. (That is one breath.)

3) Exhale and repeat the procedure using the left shoulder.

4) Repeat continuously, so the movement flows. Inhale on the right shoulder roll, breathing in oxygen to energize your system; exhale on the left shoulder roll, releasing any toxins, tensions or negativity.

5) Find a steady rhythm and keep circling the shoulders backward. Now, start leading with your elbows instead of your shoulders. Continue this movement for 20–30 seconds.

6) Now start leading with your hands, as if you're swimming the back-stroke. Remember to inhale on the right, exhale on the left. Continue this movement for 1–2 minutes.

This exercise elevates the heart rate and relaxes the tension through the shoulders and back, thus opening up the heart.

Variation: Change the direction of the shoulder rolls to a forward roll leading to a full arm front-stroke movement.

• *Yoga Posture: The Cobra* •

1) Lie on your stomach, head turned to the side. Relax your arms and hands by your side. Breathe regularly.

2) Turn your head to the front, resting your forehead on the floor. Place your hands on the floor directly beneath you shoulders. Keep your arms close to your side.

Figure 8. The Cobra.

3) Inhale, lift your upper body up slowly and carefully, bending backward in one smooth movement. Breathe regularly and continue arching the rest of your spine, keeping your hips against the floor.

4) When you've arched your back as far as you comfortably can (please do not force!) hold the position. Remember to keep breathing.

5) When you are ready to release your position, then very slowly and with controlled movement, lower yourself back to the floor, starting with your abdomen, chest, chin, nose, and forehead. Breathe in sync with the movements.

6) Relax your arms and hands beside you. Turn your head to the side and relax.

Chakra Therapies for the
5TH CHAKRA

Nature Therapy
Walk outside and become aware of the light, transparent blue color of a cloudless sky, sensing its openness and perfection. Now, look into a nearby body of water and observe the reflection of the blue sky in the crystal clear, calm waters. Sense the peace and the magnificence. If you're on the beach, watch the waves rolling on the ocean. Embrace the power and undeniable truth that is yours to express, honestly and with clarity.

Sound Therapy
New age music containing echo effects will help clear and expand the 5th chakra. Music or songs rich in high tones will stimulate and cleanse the 5th chakra as well as the clairaudient channels, which connect the throat to the ears, opening you up to your ability to hear the truth as well as speak it.

Vocally you can chant "eh" or you can sing it in the key of G. To locate "eh," start singing "ah" and gradually change it to "ee." In the middle you will find "eh." It may take a couple of tries, but you will locate the vowel sound.

Color Therapy

A light and clear shade of blue or sky blue is used for the 5th chakra. This color calms, soothes, and expands the 5th chakra, opening you up to spiritual insights and truths. I have also experienced the color of this chakra to be a light turquoise, which combines the aspect of blue sky (heaven/spirit) and the green earth. Remember, there are no rights or wrongs, these are just guidelines to follow as you experience enough to come to your own conclusions.

Aromatherapy

Scents used to calm, cool, cleanse, and purify the 5th chakra are eucalyptus, myrrh, lilac, sage, and orange flower.

Reflexology

Locate the pressure point at the base of your big toe, where the ball of the foot meets the big toe. Gently massage the point, applying steady pressure to release the blocks in the energy.

Gemstones and Crystals

Aquamarine, Azurite, Blue Lace Agate, Blue Topaz, Chalcedony, Chrysocolla, Kyanite, Lapis Lazuli, Sapphire, Sodalite, Turquoise.

• *Transformational Qualities of Gemstones and Crystals* •

AQUAMARINE: Calms nervous tension, reduces retention of body fluids and helps with digestion; increases clarity and facilitates creative self-expression; helps drive away fears and anxiety.; soothes, calms, and tranquilizes; wonderful stone to use with meditation; creates balance on all levels—physical, emotional, and mental.

AZURITE: Helps your body use oxygen in a more efficient manner; removes negative mental states and decreases stress, anxiety, and depression; facilitates peaceful meditation, opening the door for personal transformation; improves communication with Self and others; dissolves illusion; heightens psychic awareness.

BLUE LACE AGATE: Helps you gently open and expand your awareness; if you are introverted, this will help bring you out of yourself and assist you with feeling more comfortable and connected with others' environment; enhances your creativity and spontaneous, confident expression of yourself; calms the mind, soothes the emotions, and encourages clear communication inspiring wisdom, patience, kindness, and honesty; helps relieve the effect of depression, hopelessness, rigidity, and emotional upset.

BLUE TOPAZ: Strengthens the thyroid gland, boosts metabolism, and enhances mental clarity and emotional healing; provides cooling, soothing energy for your throat, facilitates creativity and honest self-expression; enhances your intuition and clearer communication with your Higher Self.

CHALCEDONY: White-blue chalcedony has a positive effect on your thyroid gland; it exerts a calming and balancing influence on the mind and reduces irritability and hypersensitivity; opens the door to inner inspiration and stimulates creative self-expression through speech or writing.

CHRYSOCOLLA: Aids in the prevention of ulcers, soothes digestive problems and symptoms of arthritis; increases your ability to maintain physical exercise, stimulates your mental abilities; diminishes fear, guilt, and tension; helps you release unconscious energy blocks; awakens feminine energies, expands your throat chakra; prompts creative expression, personal power, clear communication, and emotional stability.

KYANITE: Renews and stabilizes your throat chakra; makes it easier for you to express creatively, and communicate honestly and truthfully with serenity; facilitates out-of-body experiences also known as astral or inter-dimensional travel.

LAPIS LAZULI: Reduces tension and anxiety; revitalizes and opens your throat chakra; increases your strength and vitality; facilitates mental awareness and clear-headedness; enhances psychic abilities and communication with your Higher Self.

SAPPHIRE: Integrates body, mind, and spirit; aids clear and easy communication; enhances psychic abilities, creative expression, and connection with your Higher Self; strengthens will; expands cosmic awareness; dissolves mental confusion, nervous anxiety, and other negative mental states; helps relieve symptoms of asthma and other throat disorders.

SODALITE: Balances the male and female polarities within; stills and clears the mind, releasing and balancing mental confusion; has a tranquilizing and grounding influence; dissolves illusion, bringing clarity and truth to light; enhances communication and creative expression; similar qualities to Lapis Lazuli.

TURQUOISE: Vitalizes and fortifies your entire body; helps circulation, lungs, and both the nervous and respiratory systems; enhances meditation, creative expression, tranquillity, emotional balance, and clear communication; attracts positive energy and protects against negative influences; blends the higher purpose of the spirit with the primordial life energy of our planet (blue of the sky combined with the green of the earth); attracts abundance and prosperity.

Yoga Therapy

The yoga practice for the 5th chakra is Mantra Yoga. A mantra is an incantation—a mystical sound repeated to provide a form of meditation. It may be voiced aloud or thought inwardly. The mantra is repeated hundreds, even thousands of times. The outward vocalization of a mantra has been popularized by the teaching of "guru" Maharishi Mahesh Yogi, affiliated with Transcendental Meditation (TM), which is a streamlined form of Mantra Yoga. When sounded aloud, mantras are repeated in a voice that is alive and resonant—not a voice that is empty, dull, or mechanical. The aim of Mantra Yoga is to utilize the power of sound vibrations to influence different states of conscious awareness.

After chanting the mantra, one concentrates and listens to the internal sounds until achieving the heightened state of awareness. The most famous and powerful mantra is AUM which becomes OM when voiced.

• *Recommended Yoga Postures* •

THYROID: Pose of Tranquillity, Child Pose, Spinal Twist, Sun Salutation

DEPRESSION: Sun Salutation, Pose of Tranquillity, The Cobra, Spinal Twist

THROAT: Lion

TMJ: Lion, Pose of Tranquillity, Cleansing Breath

Physical and Breathing Exercises

• *Common Physical Exercise: Shoulder Shrugs* •

While standing or sitting up straight, chest open, shoulders relaxed:

1) Inhale and lift your shoulders up toward your ears.

2) Hold for a few seconds and release, exhaling as the shoulders return to the starting position.

3) Repeat 5 times.

4) Then gently, carefully lower your right ear toward your right shoulder.

5) Hold the position 15–30 seconds, breathing regularly.

6) Repeat on the other side, lowering left ear to left shoulder.

7) Lower your chin toward your chest and hold the position 15–30 seconds, gently stretching the back of the neck and top of the back. Breathe regularly.

8) Return your head to "normal," relaxed position.

9) Repeat Steps 1–8 one more time.

• *Yoga Posture: The Lion* •

Please position yourself in any comfortable position for this exercise.

1) Inhale and draw in a slow deep breath.

2) Exhale as you open your eyes and mouth as wide as possible.

3) Slowly, stick out your tongue as far as it will go without straining (see figure 9).

4) Hold the position as long as your exhalation lasts, then slowly relax your tongue and facial muscles.

5) Continue breathing and visualizing all tension draining away from your face and throat.

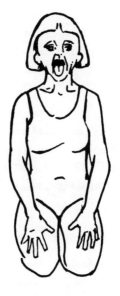

Figure 9. The Lion.

Chakra Therapies for the
6TH CHAKRA

Nature Therapy

Find a location where the city lights don't interfere with star-gazing. If you can be in the mountains where you're closer to the stars, that's even better. Now, just contemplate the starry, deep-blue night sky; let the magic and expansiveness of the stars in the sky remind you of your limitless potentials, and let it fill you with insight and dreams of reaching for the stars.

Sound Therapy

Listening to new age music or classical music, particularly Bach or Mozart, helps to open the 6th chakra. I have heard of studies that suggest those who listen to Mozart significantly increase their IQ. I don't know for a fact if that's true, but it is something to ponder.

Vocally, you can chant "e" as in "easy" or sing it in the key of A.

Color Therapy

Transparent, indigo blue is used for the 6th chakra because it has an opening and purifying effect on the chakra. Colors also found in the 6th chakra that indicate different functions are yellow (representing higher intellectual thought), clear dark blue (indicating intuition and holistic knowledge), and violet (representing abilities for extrasensory perception).

Aromatherapy

Scents used to purify and cleanse the 6th chakra are lavender, gardenia, mint, rosemary, and jasmine. These activate the senses and assist in gaining a new perspective on things, and help you see clearly what's happening around you.

Reflexology

Locate the pressure point in the fleshy mound in the middle of your big toe. Pressing gently, stimulate the release of blocks by massaging the area in a circular motion.

Gemstones and Crystals

Amethyst, Ametrine, Azurite, Blue Topaz, Indicolite Tourmaline, Kyanite, Lapis Lazuli, Quartz Crystal, Sapphire, Sodalite, Sugilite.

• *Transformational Qualities of Gemstones and Crystals* •

AMETHYST: Energizes and purifies the blood system and relieves mental confusion; cleanses and renews all levels of consciousness; dissolves illusion, enhances intuition, encourages deep meditation, and transformation; helps protect from negative influences; increases ability to heal and experience Divine love.

AMETRINE: Used for accessing your higher wisdom through meditation; uses the higher information on the earth plane to ground you; brings more stability and harmony into your life; eases headache pain and depression; combines qualities of amethyst and citrine.

AZURITE: Helps your body use oxygen in a more efficient manner; removes negative mental states and decreases stress, anxiety, and depression; facilitates peaceful meditation, opening the door for personal transformation; improves communication with Self and others; dissolves illusion; heightens psychic awareness.

BLUE TOPAZ: Strengthens the thyroid gland, boosts metabolism, and enhances mental clarity and emotional healing; provides cooling, soothing energy for your throat; facilitates creativity and honest self-expression; enhances your intuition and communication with your Higher Self.

INDICOLITE TOURMALINE: Facilitates penetrating insights and an ability to reclaim and unify your energy and personal power; assists with letting go of fear and inhibitions; encourages listening to your higher wisdom, and discerning the truth by cutting though illusion; enhances patience, serenity, intuition, and self-confidence.

KYANITE: Renews and stabilizes your throat chakra; makes it easier to express creatively and communicate honestly and truthfully with serenity; facilitates out-of-body experiences, also known as astral or interdimensional travel.

LAPIS LAZULI: Reduces tension and anxiety; revitalizes and opens your throat chakra; increases strength and vitality; facilitates mental awareness and clear headedness; enhances psychic abilities and communication with your Higher Self.

QUARTZ CRYSTAL (CLEAR): Increases the strength of your auric field; awakens all levels of consciousness; drives away negativity in your energy field and in your surroundings; used for meditation to enhance communication with your Higher Self; Quartz receives, energizes, stores, transmits, and magnifies energy.

SAPPHIRE: Integrates body, mind and spirit; aids clear and easy communication; enhances psychic abilities, creative expression, and connection with your Higher Self; strengthens will; expands cosmic awareness; dissolves mental confusion, nervous anxiety, and other negative mental states; helps relieve symptoms of asthma and other throat disorders.

SODALITE: Balances the male and female polarities within; stills and clears the mind, releasing and balancing mental confusion; has a tranquilizing and grounding influence; dissolves illusion, bringing clarity and truth to light; enhances communication and creative expression; similar qualities to Lapis Lazuli.

SUGILITE: Strengthens the heart and aids in the physical healing and purification of the body; helps you channel your spiritual awareness into physical action; calms emotions and reduces tension; has a strong protective quality that allows you to increase your sensitivity and awareness of your Self; facilitates deep meditation.

Yoga Therapy

There are two yogas associated with the 6th chakra—Jnana Yoga and Yantra Yoga.

Jnana Yoga is the "Yoga of Knowledge" and uses the intellect to cut through illusion to find Truth. It uses thought to find the "innermost center." Eventually, in the end, thought is stilled, quieted, and transcended. A stripping away, similar to peeling off the layers of an onion, is basic to the meditative practice of Jnana Yoga. The key question is, "Who (or what) am I?" As you discover what you are not, it is peeled away until the last layer is discarded and only the fullness of Being (God) remains.

Yantra Yoga uses yantras (forms or design symbols) as focal points for concentration. Just as a mantra (sacred word) is repeated, so a yantra is gazed upon, which focuses thought and holds the mind steady, opening it to the deeper meaning of the symbol. The diagrams are drawn for the purpose of finding the center of one's being, or Self-realization. Mandalas are the most popular and elaborate form of yantras used. Mandala is a Hindu word meaning "circle," and symbolizes unity and wholeness.

• *Recommended Yoga Postures* •

TENSION: Back Stretching, Pose of Tranquillity, Mountain Pose, Shoulder Stand

EYESTRAIN: Pose of Tranquillity, Child Pose

HEADACHE: Lion, Pose of Tranquillity

SINUSITIS: Mountain Pose, Pose of Tranquillity, Sun Salutation

Physical and Breathing Exercises

• *Common Physical Exercise: Eyes* •

While standing or sitting up straight, chest open, shoulders relaxed:

1) Cover your left eye with your left hand. Hold the index finger of your right hand about a foot in front of your face. Locate a focal point (piece of furniture, telephone pole, etc.) at least 6 feet from you.

2) Focus your right eye on your finger.

3) Switch your focus to the object in the distance.

4) Repeat this 5 times.

5) Repeat Steps 1–3 using your left eye (covering your right eye with right hand).

6) Repeat 5 times.

7) Then, inhale and open your eyes as wide as they'll go. Exhale and close your eyes tight. Repeat 5 times.

8) Relax.

• *Yoga Posture: Palming* •

1) Sit up tall, spine comfortably erect, at a table or desk where you can also rest your elbows.

2) Rub the palms of your hands together, briskly, warming them and charging them with natural electricity.

3) Gently place your palms (fingers together to block the light) over your closed eyes. Rest your fingers slightly on your forehead. Relax your eyelids, avoiding placing any pressure on the eyeballs. Breathe regularly.

Figure 10. Palming.

4) Stay in this position for 1–2 minutes.

5) Separate your fingers and open your eyes to let your eyes adjust to the light. Relax your arms and hands. Blink your eyes a few times to help get you back into your body.

6) Repeat, if you'd like. This exercise helps relieve eyestrain.

Chakra Therapies for the
7TH CHAKRA

Nature Therapy
Spend time alone on the top of a mountain in quiet contemplation. The top of a mountain is the highest place you can physically go to connect with God to experience the magnificence and interconnectedness of the universe.

Sound Therapy
Listen to any music that will lead you to silence, for silence is the therapy for the 7th chakra. Stilling the mind lets you hear the guidance and know the wisdom of the Divine.

Vocally you can chant "m" or sing it in the key of B. A mantra for the 7th chakra is AUM sounded as OM, a sacred syllable representing the Absolute.

Color Therapy
Violet is used for the 7th chakra to facilitate a transformation of mind and soul, opening both to the spiritual dimensions of being. You can also use white, which contains all the colors of the spectrum, assists in integrating the different levels of life into a higher purpose, and opens us to Divine light, knowledge, and healing.

Gold is also a color of the 7th chakra, and has aspects similar to white but with less intensity. Gold is the highest vibration that the physical body can tolerate for extended periods of time without "frying" (feeling spaced-out).

Aromatherapy
Scents used to restore, stimulate, and integrate the energies of the 7th chakra are lotus, clove, peppermint, olibanum, and cinnamon.

Reflexology
Locate the pressure points at the very top of the big toe and also the top of the toe next to it. Massage in a circular motion, applying steady pressure, to stimulate the 7th chakra energies and remove any blocks.

Gemstones and Crystals
Alexandrite, Amethyst, Ametrine, Citrine, Diamond, Purple Fluorite, Rock Crystal, Selenite, Sugilite.

• *Transformational Properties of Gemstones and Crystals* •

ALEXANDRITE: Aids internal and external regeneration; has positive influence on nervous system, spleen, pancreas; helps align mental and emotional body; aids spiritual transformation and regeneration; reflects highest potentials of unfoldment; stimulates happiness and pleasant surprises, joy, oneness with life.

AMETHYST: Energizes and purifies the blood system, and relieves mental confusion; cleanses and renews all levels of consciousness; dissolves illusion, enhances intuition, encourages deep meditation and transformation; helps protect from negative influences; increases ability to heal and experience Divine love.

AMETRINE: Used for accessing your higher wisdom through meditation, and using the higher information on the earth plane to ground you; brings more stability and harmony into your life; eases headache pain and depression; combines qualities of amethyst and citrine.

CITRINE: Excellent stone for healing ailments of the kidneys, heart, digestive organs, colon, and liver; helps body eliminate toxins; reduces self-destructive behavior and instills a feeling of stability; elevates self-esteem and enhances alignment with your Higher Self; attracts abundance, and helps you ground to the present time.

DIAMOND: Enhances higher mental abilities; holds master healing vibration that, when used in conjunction with other gems, intensifies their healing power; dissolves negativity; purifies your physical body and auric field; intensifies and activates the "god-like" aspects within.

PURPLE FLUORITE: Grounds excess energy; advances the intellect, promotes greater concentration and deeper meditation; helps you to understand the higher, more abstract metaphysical concepts, and facilitates clearer communication with your Higher Self; holds powerful healing vibrations that offer a deep sense of comfort and tranquillity.

SUGILITE: Strengthens the heart and aids in physical healing and purification of the body; helps channel your spiritual awareness into physical actions; calms emotions and reduces tension; has a strong protective quality that allows you to increase your sensitivity and awareness of your Self; facilitates deep meditation.

Yoga Therapy
All forms of Yoga lead to the opening of the 7th chakra, to the awakening of your higher consciousness, the experience of "oneness with the universe," and the divinity of all creation.

• *Recommended Yoga Postures* •

IMMUNE SYSTEM: Pose of Tranquillity, Spinal Twist, Sun Salutation, The Tree

Physical and Breathing Exercises

• *Common Physical Exercise: Rubbing the Top of Your Head* •

While in a comfortable position, gently rub the top of your head in a circular direction to the right. This stimulates the blood flow and assists with opening the 7th chakra. Do this for 15 seconds.

• *Yoga Posture: Pose of Tranquillity* •

1) Lie full length on your back, legs extended (but not rigid), with your feet a comfortable distance apart, and each foot falling limply outward (see figure 11).

2) Relax your arms by your sides, a comfortable distance from your body. Release any tension from your hands.

3) Focus on your breathing, taking nice deep breaths from the abdomen. Inhale, breathing in positive, cleansing energy, and exhale, releasing any tension or toxins.

4) When your breathing has settled into a smooth, light, rhythmic action, start to focus your full attention on individual body parts so that tension in each area just drains away, leaving the body totally relaxed. One way of doing this is by first tensing (contracting the muscles in) each body part, holding the tension, and then releasing it (called the contraction and relaxation method of stretching).

The sequence of relaxation is as follows: start with your feet and work your way up through the body to the head: feet, calves, front of thighs, back of thighs, pelvis, abdomen, lower back, chest, upper back, fingers, hands, forearms, upper arms—front and back, shoulders, throat, neck, jaw, lips, tongue, eyes, brow, and scalp.

Figure 11. Pose of Tranquillity.

5) Continue focusing on your breathing, quieting the mind. Scan your body once more for tension, breathing into areas that may still be holding tension.

6) Hold this position for as long as your time allows.

Part Three

EXERCISING
YOUR
CHAKRAS

An Exercise Series for Opening the Chakras

The following is a set of toning, flexibility, and breathing exercises that produce an energizing effect on the chakras. When this series is practiced daily, the results are invigorating. You may notice that the energy builds subtly, exercise to exercise, chakra to chakra, until there is a release in the final exercise which corresponds to the 7th chakra. The first three exercises emphasize physical strength and movement. Exercises 4–7 are gentle, emphasizing stretching flexibility.

Wide-Stance Plié with a Pelvic Rock
1ST CHAKRA

The color for this chakra is a vibrant, clear red.

1) Stand with your feet wider than shoulder-width apart as shown in figure 12 on page 148. Toes are facing outward, in a plié position. Make sure your knees are in alignment with your ankles to avoid stressing the knee joints. The weight is over the back of your heels (not your toes).

Figure 12. Wide-stance plié with a pelvic rock.

2) Place your hands on your hips and start lowering your hips by bending at your knees as if you are performing a squat or deep knee bend. As you lower your hips, pause and *inhale*, contracting your abdominal muscles and tilting the pelvis forward. Hold. Then *exhale*, releasing the tension in the abdominals and gently press the pelvis to the back.

3) Repeat this rocking motion 3 times on the way down (3rd time being at the lowest position) and then 3 times as you come back to a standing position.

4) Repeat this entire sequence at least 3 times.

Squat with Hip Circle
2ND CHAKRA

The color for this chakra is clear orange.

1) Stand with your feet shoulder-width apart, toes facing forward, knees are slightly bent, weight is over your heels. Make sure your knees are in alignment with your ankles (directly over) to avoid stressing the knee joints.

2) As in the first exercise, inhale as you contract the abdominal muscles and tilt the pelvis forward; exhale as you press it back (see figure 13). Repeat this several times.

3) Slowly rotate your hips in a circle: *inhale* as you tilt the pelvis forward, *exhale* shifting your weight to the right hip; *inhale* as you shift the weight to the back (buttocks), *exhale* as you shift the weight to the left hip.

4) Repeat this circular motion to the right at least 3 times.

5) Change directions, rotating the hip circles to the left. Repeat 3 times.

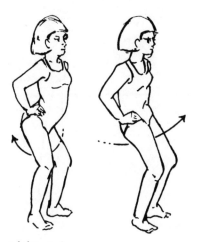

Figure 13. Squat with hip circle.

Jumping for Joy!
3RD CHAKRA

The color for the 3rd chakra is bright, sunny yellow.

1) Start with your feet a comfortable distance apart and jump up and down, bringing your knees as close to your chest as possible. Keep your knees slightly bent as you land to avoid stressing the knee joints. Do this for several minutes.

2) Rest. Then repeat.

Suggestion: Using a mini-trampoline for this is great and lots of fun, too! If you have a willing partner, he or she can support you while you jump, as shown in figure 14.

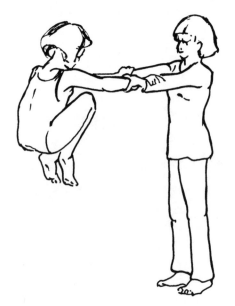

Figure 14. Jumping for Joy!

Modified Cobra Leading into Child Pose
4TH CHAKRA

The colors for the 4th chakra are pink and green.

1) Lie face down on the floor. Legs are extended. Place your hands chest level, shoulder-width apart (as if you were going to do a push-up).

2) Head facing forward, gently lift your upper back, arching the spine slowly and carefully as far as you comfortably can! Keep your hips in contact with the floor. This is the Cobra Position shown in figure 8, on page 127.

3) Hold the position and breathe regularly.

4) Slowly release your position, lowering your chest almost to the floor.

Figure 15. Modified Cobra leading into Child Pose.

5) Push against the floor with your hands to help raise your hips. Keeping your knees on the floor, straighten your arms and push your hips and buttocks back over your heels, so you are resting in a fetal-like position (arms in front of you, resting on the floor, with head turned to the side or forehead on the floor). See figure 15 on page 151.

6) Breathe into the stretch.

7) When you're ready, move your arms and place them by your sides, palms facing up. Breathe regularly.

8) Stay in this position for as long as you are comfortable.

9) When you're ready, round up into a kneeling position, sitting up straight, spine comfortably erect. Ready for the next exercise.

Head and Neck Rolls
5TH CHAKRA

The color for this chakra is clear, light blue.

If you are comfortable in the kneeling position from the last exercise, please remain in that position. If your knees hurt, please adjust yourself so you are comfortable.

1) Sit up straight, spine comfortably erect, head facing forward.

2) *Inhale* and gently tilt your head backward. *Exhale* and lower your chin to your chest (see figure 16).

3) Repeat this several times. (Please be very gentle with yourself.)

4) *Inhale* and gently turn your head to look over your right shoulder. *Exhale* and turn your head to look over your left shoulder.

5) Repeat this several times.

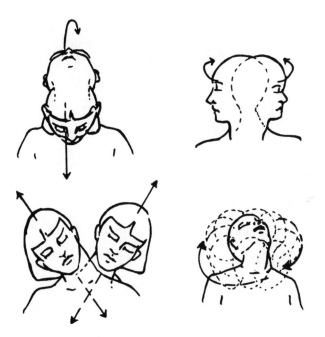

Figure 16. Head and neck rolls.

6) *Inhale* and lift your chin up and to the right. *Exhale* and lower your chin down and to the left.

7) Reverse the process: *Inhale* and lift your chin up and to the left. *Exhale* and lower your chin to the right.

8) Repeat Steps 6—7 several times.

9) Finally, very slowly and carefully, roll your neck and head all the way around in a circle several times. Pause and breathe into areas that are tense.

10) Reverse directions.

Eye Rolls

6TH CHAKRA

The color for this chakra is clear indigo blue.

Pretend you are looking at a clock and move your eyes in the following directions:

1) 12 o'clock position to 6 o'clock. Repeat several times.

2) 9 o'clock position to 3 o'clock. Repeat several times.

3) 2 o'clock position to 8 o'clock. Repeat several times.

4) 10 o'clock position to 4 o'clock. Repeat several times.

5) All the numbers going clockwise. Repeat several times.

6) All the numbers going counter clockwise. Repeat several times.

Mock Head Stand

7TH CHAKRA

The color for this chakra is violet.

If you have neck pain, please use an alternate exercise from the previous section.

1) While in the kneeling position, toes pointing backward, lean forward and rest your forehead on the floor close to your knees.

2) Hold on to your heels or ankles and *carefully* raise your buttocks away from your heels until the top of your head rests on the mat as shown in figure 17. (Do not force or exert pressure on your head or neck!)

Figure 17. Mock head stand.

3) Hold the position for only a few seconds when you start doing this exercise.

4) Ease yourself out of this posture by slowly coming back onto your heels. Keep your head low for a few seconds to "get your bearings" before sitting upright on your heels.

Bibliography and Recommended Reading

Aromatherapy

Cooksley, Valerie Gennari. *Aromatherapy: A Lifetime Guide to Healing with Essential Oils.* Englewood Cliffs, NJ: Prentice Hall, 1996.

Lavabre, Marcel. *Aromatherapy Workbook.* Rochester, VT: Healing Arts Press, 1990.

Maple, Eric. *The Magic of Perfume: Aromatics and their Esoteric Significance.* York Beach, ME: Samuel Weiser, 1973.

Rose, Jeanne. *The Aromatherapy Book: Applications and Inhalation.* Berkeley, CA: North Atlantic Books, 1992.

Chakras and Healing

Bek, Lilla and Philippa Pullar. *Healing with Chakra Energy: Restoring the Natural Harmony of the Body.* Rochester, VT: Destiny Books, 1995.

Brennan, Barbara Ann. *Hands of Light : A Guide to Healing Through the Human Energy Field.* New York: Bantam, 1987.

———. *Light Emerging: The Journey of Personal Healing.* New York: Bantam, 1993.

Landsdowne, Zachary F. *The Chakras and Esoteric Healing*. York Beach, ME: Samuel Weiser, 1986.

Marciniak, Barbara. *Bringers of the Dawn: Teachings from the Pleiadians*. Santa Fe, NM: Bear & Company, 1992.

Myss, Caroline. *Anatomy of the Spirit*. New York: Harmony Books, 1996.

Northrup, Christiane. *Women's Bodies, Women's Wisdom*. New York: Bantam, 1994.

Redfield, James. *The Celestine Prophecy: An Adventure*. New York: Warner, 1993.

Roman, Sanaya. *Personal Power through Awareness*. Tiburon, CA: H.J. Kramer, 1986.

———. *Spiritual Growth: Being Your Higher Self*. Tiburon, CA: H.J. Kramer, 1989.

Sharamon, Shalila and Bodo J. Baginski. *The Chakra Handbook*. Wilmot, WI: Lotus Light/Shangri-la, 1991.

Shell Bdolak, Levenah. *The Aura Coloring Book*. Agoura, CA: Voyant, 1990.

———. *Eco-Spirit: A Spiritual Guide to Healing the Planet*. Agoura, CA: Voyant, 1991.

Stevens, Jose. *Earth to Tao: Michael's Guide to Healing and Spiritual Awakening*. Santa Fe, NM: Bear & Company, 1989.

Wallace, Amy and Bill Henkin. *The Psychic Healing Book*. Oakland, CA: Wingbow Press, 1978.

Crystals and Gemstones

Chase, Pamela Louise and Jonathan Pawlik. *The Newcastle Guide to Healing with Gemstones: How to Use Over Seventy Different Gemstone Energies*. North Hollywood, CA: Newcastle, 1989.

Cohen, Neil. *Crystal Awareness Guide: The Transformational Properties of Gems and Minerals*. Mount Shasta, CA: Legion of Light, 1990.

Raphaell, Katrina. *Crystal Enlightenment*. Santa Fe, NM: Aurora Press, 1985.

Stein, Diane. *Healing with Gemstones and Crystals*. Freedom, CA: The Crossing Press, 1996.

Whitaker, Charlene. *Gems of Wisdom*. Canoga, CA: Cosmic Connection, 1987.

Zupsicsk, Jan. *The Rainbow Card Series: The Rainbow of Chakra Centers: Our Body-Mind Healing Tools*. Tampa, FL: Inner Light Resources, 1991.

Yoga

Frost, Gavin and Yvonne. *Tantric Yoga: The Royal Path to Raising Kundalini Power*. York Beach, ME: Samuel Weiser, 1989.

Hewitt, James. *Complete Yoga Book*. New York: Schocken Books, 1977.

Iyengar, B. K. S. *Light on Yoga*. New York: Schocken Books, 1966.

———. *The Tree of Yoga*. Boston: Shambhala, 1989.

Myers, Esther. *Yoga and You: Energizing and Relaxing Yoga for New and Experienced Students*. Boston: Shambhala, 1996.

Schiffmann, Erich. *Yoga: The Spirit and Practice of Moving Into Stillness*. New York: Pocket Books/Simon & Schuster, 1996.

Weller, Stella. *Yoga Therapy*. London: Thorsons, 1995.

Yoga Videos

Yoga Journal's Yoga Practice for Beginners. Venice, CA: Healing Arts Publishing, 1990.

Yoga Journal's Yoga Practice for Flexibility. Venice, CA: Healing Arts Publishing, 1992.

Yoga Journal's Yoga Practice for Relaxation. Venice, CA: Healing Arts Publishing, 1992.

Total Yoga. Venice, CA: Healing Arts, White Lotus Foundation, 1995.

Recommended Audio Tapes and CD's

Benedictine Monks of Santo Domingo de Silos. *Chant II*. New York: Angel Records, 1995.

Highstein, Max. *The Healer's Touch: Healing Music for Piano, Winds, Strings and Synthesizer*. Upland, CA: Search for Serenity, 1986.

Jones, Michael. *Pianoscapes: Piano Solos*. Milwaukee, WI: Narada Productions, 1985.

————. *Seascapes: Piano Solos.* Milwaukee, WI: Narada Productions, 1984.

The Lazaris Material: Lazaris Remembers Lemuria. Fairfax, CA: Concept: Synergy, 1985.

Nature Recordings. *The Sounds of Nature: The Sea, Mountain Stream, Thunderstorm in the Big Sur Mountains, Dawn and Dusk in the Ventana Wilderness.* Pacific Grove, CA: Nature Recordings, 1985.

NorthSound. *Ocean Music.* Minocqua, WI, NorthWord Press, 1994.

Shankar, Ravi. *Chants of India.* New York: Angel Records, 1997.

————. *In Celebration.* New York: Angel Records, 1995.

Additional
Answer
Sheets

ANSWER SHEET

?#	1st		2nd		3rd		4th		5th		6th		7th	
	yes	no	yes	no	yes	no	yes	no	yes	no	yes	no	yes	no
1	❑	❑									❑	❑		
2	❑	❑												
3	❑	❑												
4	❑	❑												
5	❑	❑												
6	❑	❑	❑	❑										
7	❑	❑	❑	❑										
8	❑	❑	❑	❑										
9	❑	❑	❑	❑										
10	❑	❑												
11	❑	❑					❑	❑						
12	❑	❑	❑	❑			❑	❑						
13	❑	❑												
14	❑	❑												
15	❑	❑												
16	❑	❑												
17	❑	❑												
18			❑	❑										
19			❑	❑										
20			❑	❑										
'yeses' per column														

?#	1st		2nd		3rd		4th		5th		6th		7th	
	yes	no	yes	no	yes	no	yes	no	yes	no	yes	no	yes	no
21			☐	☐										
22			☐	☐			☐	☐						
23a							☐	☐						
23b			☐	☐										
23c					☐	☐								
23d	☐	☐	☐	☐										
24			☐	☐										
25			☐	☐										
26			☐	☐										
27			☐	☐										
28			☐	☐										
29			☐	☐										
30a	☐	☐	☐	☐										
30b			☐	☐										
30c			☐	☐	☐	☐								
31a	☐	☐			☐	☐								
31b			☐	☐	☐	☐								
31c			☐	☐	☐	☐								
31d			☐	☐	☐	☐								
32			☐	☐	☐	☐								
33					☐	☐								
"yeses" per column														

?#	1st		2nd		3rd		4th		5th		6th		7th	
	yes	no	yes	no	yes	no	yes	no	yes	no	yes	no	yes	no
34					☐	☐								
35					☐	☐								
36					☐	☐								
37					☐	☐	☐	☐						
38					☐	☐								
39					☐	☐								
40					☐	☐								
41					☐	☐								
42					☐	☐								
43					☐	☐	☐	☐						
44					☐	☐								
45					☐	☐								
46					☐	☐								
47					☐	☐								
48							☐	☐						
49							☐	☐						
50							☐	☐						
51							☐	☐						
52			☐	☐			☐	☐						
53							☐	☐						
54							☐	☐						
'yeses' per column														

?#	1st		2nd		3rd		4th		5th		6th		7th	
	yes	no	yes	no	yes	no	yes	no	yes	no	yes	no	yes	no
55							☐	☐						
56							☐	☐						
57			☐	☐			☐	☐						
58							☐	☐						
59							☐	☐						
60							☐	☐						
61							☐	☐						
62							☐	☐						
63							☐	☐						
64									☐	☐				
65			☐	☐					☐	☐				
66									☐	☐				
67									☐	☐				
68									☐	☐				
69									☐	☐				
70									☐	☐				
71									☐	☐				
72							☐	☐	☐	☐				
73									☐	☐				
74			☐	☐					☐	☐				
75			☐	☐					☐	☐				
"yeses" per column														

?#	1st		2nd		3rd		4th		5th		6th		7th	
	yes	no	yes	no	yes	no	yes	no	yes	no	yes	no	yes	no
76			☐	☐					☐	☐				
77			☐	☐					☐	☐				
78					☐	☐			☐	☐				
79							☐	☐	☐	☐				
80									☐	☐				
81									☐	☐				
82							☐	☐	☐	☐				
83											☐	☐		
84											☐	☐		
85											☐	☐		
86											☐	☐		
87	☐	☐									☐	☐		
88			☐	☐							☐	☐		
89											☐	☐		
90											☐	☐		
91											☐	☐		
92											☐	☐		
93											☐	☐		
94											☐	☐	☐	☐
95	☐	☐									☐	☐		
96											☐	☐	☐	☐
"yeses" per column														

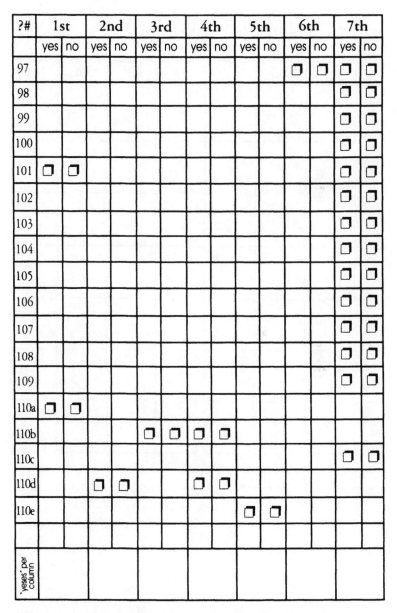

?#	1st		2nd		3rd		4th		5th		6th		7th	
	yes	no	yes	no	yes	no	yes	no	yes	no	yes	no	yes	no
97											❏	❏	❏	❏
98													❏	❏
99													❏	❏
100													❏	❏
101	❏	❏											❏	❏
102													❏	❏
103													❏	❏
104													❏	❏
105													❏	❏
106													❏	❏
107													❏	❏
108													❏	❏
109													❏	❏
110a	❏	❏												
110b					❏	❏	❏	❏						
110c													❏	❏
110d			❏	❏			❏	❏						
110e									❏	❏				
'yeses' per column														

*Note: A number of questions relate to several chakras. The chakras listed on the answer sheet are the chakras *most* affected. (Although other chakras may be affected to a lesser degree they have not been noted on the answer sheet.)

ANSWER SHEET TALLY

	1st	2nd	3rd	4th	5th	6th	7th
page 1 'yes' answers							
page 2 'yes' answers							
page 3 'yes' answers							
page 4 'yes' answers							
page 5 'yes' answers							
page 6 'yes' answers							
TOTAL all 6 pages							

Index |

About the Author

Deedre Diemer is a nationally acclaimed intuitive counselor, speaker, and seminar leader. For over a decade, Deedre has assisted people in creating immediate and profound life changes in their relationships and self-images. Outgoing and charismatic, Deedre Diemer is a true "student of life," having spent the last twenty years actively involved with personal growth and development. She holds a Master's Degree in psychology from the University of Santa Monica, and also spent two years studying the healing arts at the Intuitive Arts Center in California. She furthered her education in the mind/body connection through extensive study as the Transpersonal Hypnotherapy Institute in Boulder, Colorado, where she received certification as a hypnotherapist. Believing in the importance of balancing mind/body/spirit, Deedre is also a fitness instructor, receiving her diploma in Fitness and Nutrition from the Professional Career Development Institute in Atlanta, Georgia.

Deedre currently has a growing counseling practice in Los Angeles, and has developed her intuitive skills as a clairvoyant and psychic healer. She offers classes and lectures which integrate psychic/spiritual healing with proven, practical psychotherapeutic techniques.

Printed in the United States
205067BV00001B/234/P

5713263R0

Made in the USA
Lexington, KY
11 June 2010